The
POINT

Jon Lane

DEDICATION

To my parents, my wife, my two daughters and Rufus the dog!

I love you all.

CONTENTS

INTRODUCTION

If you have ever asked yourself "***What is the point?***" then this book could help you find an answer to that question.

The POINT is intended to help you find your own direction, to add meaning to your life and to enable you to do more of what you love. You too can reach your own summit…*thank you to my daughter Emily for the cover design!*

I hope you find the book enjoyable and interesting, and that you will take at least one positive thing from it. One thing would be just fine, and could be profound.

Best of luck as you take the next step…

WHAT IS THE POINT?

Firstly, thank you for opening this book and reading this far.

Okay, so there is a fair way to go, and I appreciate that, and I also appreciate that every journey starts with the first step, and you have done that. So congratulations, I like you already! Some say that there is a joy in the pursuit of anything, and so let's now move forward together and take another step…

What is the point? That is a very good question, and one that I have asked myself many times in the past. Can I tell you what the point is? No, I cannot, not yet. What I can do is help you to find it, and I really do need your help to do that.

Wait! Please do not put this book down now. It's true, I don't have the answer. I wish I did, and I wish it was that simple, but here's the thing…it is actually relatively simple, and the thing is, YOU have the answer. It's there, waiting.

I have called this book "The POINT" because it is intended to help you find a way ahead and the concept that I have come up with is to use each letter from the word **POINT** as a way of remembering each part. In this way I have used the word as a type of mnemonic called an acronym, to make it more memorable.

If you are doing something and ask yourself *"What is the point of doing this?"* then try to think of the acronym **POINT** and then consider each letter as I describe in this book later on, it just might help you see that usually there is a point.

You may not realise it yet, but you, and only you, have the answer to what the POINT is, and I can help you find it. Another thing is that, once you have found what the POINT is, you are able to apply it, and it will become very effective for you. Yes, there really is a point to this book after all.

Every single one of us: you, me, your friends, my dad, daughters, sons, your manager, your teacher etc. we are the only ones who really know what we want. Once we know what we want, we can start to live our lives with a clear **purpose** and way forward. This then enables us to make more sense of what we're doing, and to appreciate that most things can guide us towards what we want. This can make life a whole lot more enjoyable, and this can give you a wonderful new perspective.

I have spent many years wondering about this question, as I did throughout school and working for many different companies and businesses. Throughout my life and career, I have worked alongside family and friends and colleagues young and old. Over this time I have come to realise that, with a clear purpose, life makes a lot more sense, and it can help you to become happier.

Like it or not, we are human beings who have been born into

this world and we live here for a number of years. At some point we will die, and we have a relatively brief time here on earth in which to live. We can choose what we do, well to some extent, and all of us have the same amount of time each day to "live" eat and sleep.

In the grand scheme of things, if you consider that the age of the Earth is apparently around 4.5 Billion years, then in a way you and I are not around for long. You might as well get on with something that you enjoy, because it's quite likely that you will become very successful at it, and what's the point in doing anything else?

When you're doing something that you have to do (e.g. school), having a purpose that you are working towards can really help you understand why you're doing it. Perhaps it might become useful one day in the future when your interests develop further and your passion for mastering a particular subject area grows.

You might find that the small nugget of information that you learnt in that Geography class many years ago, suddenly makes sense and is relevant to what you do and to what makes you happy! The fact that you passed your Geography exam at school could now enable you to take the subject to the next level, in line with what you want to achieve. You are keeping your options open.

The mere process of learning helps your mind grow, work more effectively and become more adept to learning in the future. Similar to how regular exercising and stretching your muscles helps you to become stronger and more flexible, exercising your brain makes it stronger. All learning is good.

There is in fact a lot of useful learning in most things that we do.

You may just not see it yet, but perhaps in the future you will.

Please come with me and embrace this book, as I am doing now (in writing it) and I truly hope it will help you, as it has done me.

One of the things that I think you're going to love about this book is that it is simple, memorable and effective. People can discover new ways of thinking and behaving, and identify solutions to their own problems, as I'm sure you will.

The acronym **POINT** should help you to generate and maintain focus on where you are going, and to ultimately get there…

By the time you've finished reading about "**P**" you may already have changed your view on the world, and you will already be moving forward to where you want to be. This is not rocket science, no engineering qualifications are required, or helmets, this is simple and effective, anyone can do it, and in the days and weeks ahead you will see your life opening up before you, with renewed passion and interest.

Within this book I have tried to include things that have resonated with me throughout my life, and so I truly hope that some of them resonate also with you. Some say that the information contained within this book has helped them to see things differently, and that is what makes me happy and I agree that a lot of what I write about seems to help.

I really hope you enjoy this book, and I welcome any feedback, positive or negative, as all feedback is a gift.

We are getting to the **POINT**.

And now, a short story...

Jake was a curious kid who enjoyed seeing new things and exploring his surroundings. He had a mountain bike and loved to cycle around the small town where he lived, looking at new things and talking to people.

One day he met an old lady at a bus stop who told him that she had travelled many miles and visited many places in her lifetime, and that his town was special. Even though it was quite small, there was something in it that was unique and amazing, perhaps the most amazing thing in the world!

Jake was a bit surprised about that, and asked the lady where this thing was. She said that if he kept looking around the town he would definitely see it. She then turned around, and stepped into the waiting bus. He watched her sit down and then saw her peer out of the side glass window and smile at him. The bus then drove off and slowly disappeared out of view.

Stunned for a moment, Jack got back on his bike and thought about the most amazing thing in the world and wondered what it could be, and also where it could be. He'd never heard about it before. He cycled off to the library and asked if they knew what is was, and where it was. The man at the desk didn't know and said that perhaps Jake should cycle along the high street to see if it was there, so he did, but he couldn't find it. He saw a policeman, who told him to try inside the town hall, but he couldn't find it in there either, and so he went to the big park.

He walked around the park, climbed up a tree, looked around in all directions, across the town, but could not see anything that looked like the most amazing thing in the world.

He saw the shimmering pond in the middle of the park with its fountain in the middle and wondered whether that could perhaps be what the lady had referred to. It didn't seem that great to him though, and so he decided to take a rest and sit by the pond and feed the ducks with some bread that he had in his pocket.

After a while he decided that it was time to go home and that his search was over for today. He threw the rest of the bread into the water, said goodbye to the ducks and said to himself that tomorrow he would again search for the most amazing thing in the world. As he got up he glanced down into the water, saw his own reflection, smiled at himself, and went home.

P

Purpose

Be Positive

Be Proactive

People need a purpose in order to feel worthwhile. Everything has a purpose, a reason for living. If you're a spoon, it's simple, or a chair, or a guard dog perhaps, but what about if you are a human being? What is your purpose on this planet? Is it just to reproduce, or is it more than that?

It is surprising perhaps how many people really haven't thought about it much. The possibilities are endless. Ask yourself *"What is the point of my existence?"*

You were born on this earth, brought up by someone, interacted with other children, you met a lot of people as you grew up, went to school and learnt many things, but what is the point of it all?

What is your purpose on this planet? Is there anything particular that you would like to strive towards? Do you have a real interest in something or a skill that you would like to develop further?

We need to have a purpose. Without a purpose, well, there is little point in living. We could just waft about having fun and taking what we can out of life, but would that really be fulfilling?

When you're lying in bed aged 90, tired and wondering what you did in your life, what would you give to go back to today and start doing something really worthwhile?

You might not have a purpose at all, and yet when your life comes to an end you may have actually done lots of great things and achieved a lot, but did you do what you wanted to do? Why take the risk? It's surely better to be proactive and try to decide what you would like to achieve. You may come off the path a few times, but at least you can try to go along the path that you have chosen and try to pursue your own purpose in life.

When you go on holiday, you normally have a particular destination in mind that you may have arranged months in advance. As you get closer to the journey you might start thinking about how you are going to get there, and what things you are going to do when you get there. You're planning it, and typically you will get there and do some or perhaps most of the things that you had arranged to do.

Now, instead of the above, imagine that on the first day of your holiday you just got into your car and started driving away from your house without a destination. That would be weird wouldn't it? "*Where are we going*" the kids would ask excitedly, "*I haven't a clue!*" could be the reply. It might end up being a great holiday, but it also might be a disaster. Either way, you would have ended up doing something rather random and probably not what you would have ideally liked to do.

So if you have something in mind that you would like to do, then surely it would make sense to at least try? It could perhaps be the greatest purpose of all. In fact, for you it certainly will be. It doesn't matter if it's wrong because you can change it anytime you like. It is yours to create and yours to keep and it will be with you for as long as you want it to be. When you identify a purpose then you behave differently because you now have a direction, and others see that, and they can help you to achieve it. Whether they know it or not, they are likely to help you become more successful.

When you die, what would you like to see written on your tombstone? She was a lovely person? He helped others? She started a revolution? He left the world a brighter place? She created a brilliant business? He helped others every day?

The thing about knowing your own Purpose is that it is very powerful. Once you have an idea of your purpose, you will start to work towards it and you will see, hear and feel things that identify with your purpose. You will act in a purposeful way. Things that happen every day will suddenly make more sense to you, and you will quickly be able to understand what is aligned to your purpose and what is not. The more things that you do that are aligned to your purpose the more likely you will become more fulfilled.

Have you heard about the Monarch butterfly?

Well, it's a remarkable story and one that involves a journey of around three thousand miles and which spans several butterfly generations. Monarch butterflies live in the northeast United

States and Canada, but they are not able to survive the cold winters and so they migrate south-west each autumn to escape the cold.

These butterflies take to the air and fly to either Southern California or Mexico, and they somehow navigate to the same trees every year. These butterflies will never return back to their northern birthplace, and the strange thing is that they have never been to these trees before, because it was a previous generation that came here before.

In fact, the overall annual journey requires several butterfly lifetimes, as it is a round trip of around six thousand miles. Because it takes so long, the return trip alone requires three generations. Yes three generations of butterflies just to fly back to the northern starting point!

After waiting out the winter, the original butterflies take to the skies and fly part of the way back to warmer climes such as Texas where they lay their eggs. These eggs hatch into brilliantly striped caterpillars which later on transform into adult butterflies. These butterflies then take to the skies and fly another few hundred miles north, lay their eggs and the process repeats. The next generation of butterflies completes the remaining distance, lays their eggs, and it is the next generation that re-starts the process and makes the longest journey down south again.

For such slow moving and delicate creatures, this whole journey spanning four generations of butterflies is a seemingly impossible task, and yet because their purpose is somehow programmed into them, many millions of them survive and complete it.

The whole journey repeats again at the end of summer, and another fascinating aspect to this is that the generation of butterfly that has to fly the longest stretch, the journey South-west, has a longer life span. This particular generation (typically one in every four) live for eight months, which is much longer than the usual month or so that the other generations live. How is it possible for this pattern of one generation in four living longer than the others?

How these butterflies know their purpose and how it's passed on through generations is not clear, but what we do know is that because they have this single purpose they often achieve it, and that is the main point to take from this story. If you have a purpose, something to work towards, then you are very likely to achieve it.

Imagine if the butterflies all flew around randomly, it's quite unlikely that any of them would reach the same destination. And so, although we don't know why they follow this same pattern, they are proving that having a clear purpose in mind can result in success.

What is your purpose?

As you read through this book, and think about the messages and wonder how they apply to you, you might start to think of new ideas and concepts that you hadn't thought about before. Now is a good time to write down one thing that is in line with your purpose. Something that you would like to stand for.

We each need to make sense of our world and our lives in our own way, and it's important to do this. We each see the world differently, and so we have to make sense of it ourselves. Embrace what you see, hear and feel, and do what you can to live a fulfilled life, in whatever way that suits you. There is really no point in doing anything else!

You may already have started to become aware of new feelings and thoughts coming into your mind. Some say embrace these new ideas, try them out for a while, and then decide whether to keep doing them or discard them and try something else. I agree with this philosophy, as having a purpose that you believe in, and are happy with, is more important to sticking to one rigidly that you are not fully congruent with.

Some people find it helpful to ask themselves the following questions because it can help to generate ideas around their own purpose:

- What would give you a real sense of achievement?
- What would you like to contribute to the world?
- Which historical figures do you admire and why?
- What skills or personal strengths do you have?
- What makes you happy?
- How would you like to be remembered after you die?
- How would you like to be remembered after every interaction with anyone?
- In an ideal world what would your main purpose be?

I have two daughters and one of my purposes is to be a great father, and to love and support them always. We don't always see eye to eye, and occasionally I get frustrated with their mess, or if they are being noisy - I consider my purpose and then I try to guide them in a positive way, and I always try to be the best father that I can be. I find it helpful to be true to my purpose every day and perhaps it could do the same for you?

There really is no reason why you wouldn't follow your heart, and so if you can fathom out where you want to go, you are already on your way!

It's okay if you don't have a clear purpose, it will come in time. Things often just arrive in time for when they're needed.

Thinking about your own purpose and trying to focus on it in the future is proactively taking you towards where you want to be, and by doing this, you are "Making things happen". It is so much better to make things happen yourself than to wait for things to be done to you. My dad once said to me that there are three types of people in this world: Some people make things happen, some people watch things happen and some people wonder what happened. Try to be someone who makes things happen, and shape your own world.

A friend of mine placed a pot plant in front of me and said, "*What's that doing?*" "Not a lot" I replied, and he agreed that not much seemed to be happening, however something was and he again asked me what, if anything, it was doing.

I replied "*Growing*" and he agreed, yes that is what it was doing. It was growing, using its leaves to absorb sunlight for photosynthesis resulting in cell division and cell expansion. The plant was slowly, very slowly, getting bigger. His point was that it wasn't dormant. If a plant was not growing then it was dying. He was highlighting to me that it's similar to us. We need to grow, both physically and also mentally, and if we're not learning and moving forward then we are moving backwards. Your life is ending one day at a time, and so try to make the most of what time you have, and try to learn at least one thing each and every day.

Steve Jobs (the founder of Apple) went to college but dropped out and decided to try a Calligraphy class because it sounded fun and he loved it. He learned all about serif and sans serif typefaces, varying the amount of space between different letter combinations and about typography. At that time he had no use for it, however, 10 years later, when he was developing the first Apple Macintosh it all came back to him and he incorporated much of what he had learnt.

Sometimes when you look back on your own life, the things that you did in the past (that seemed so irrelevant at the time) connect up, and often make sense later on. It makes me smile to think about his contribution to the world as I type this now on my Apple iMac!

Another thing that Steve Jobs used to do each morning was to look into the mirror and ask himself the following question: *"If today were the last day of my life, would I do what I'm about to do today?"* Whenever the answer was "No" for too many days in a row, he knew he would need to change something.

It's really important to try to enjoy each day and although some days might not start out great or can be very challenging, it's usually possible to generate at least one moment of enjoyment. If that is not the case for you, then change something. This is the only chance you will have on earth, with this exciting adventure called life. So why not plan it, and try to live it as richly and as happily as possible?

Before moving on to "O" I wanted to also mention one more "P" which is "Being **P**ositive". It really is important to have a positive attitude to things because usually they will turn out all right in the end, and you never know what the alternative might have been.

It might be annoying when the bus is late, however if it had been a bit earlier then it might have had an accident. Or when you fall and break your arm, at least you didn't fall on your face and break your nose too (hopefully). It really is true, you never know what might have happened instead of what did happen, and it really could be a whole lot worse. What's done is done and is in the past, all that you can do is be here now, and to embrace the future. The main person who is impacted if you are negative is you, and so why harm yourself? Pick yourself up, dust yourself down and move on, positively.

If you can, shrug your shoulders (assuming they're not broken!) and try to move on with a smile. If you think about it, there are so many good things that happen in our lives that we tend to take them for granted, and it's a shame to dwell on the occasional negatives. Being positive and trying to have a strong attitude is really good for you, and your body language will show this to all around you. Other people will see this and be more positive back to you. Positivity breeds positivity…smile and the world smiles too.

Some people have a view that every action has a positive intention, and I think that this is a nice way to view the world. It's hard to believe sometimes, but in some ways I do agree with it.

Bizarre as it seems, when someone does something hurtful to you, or shouts at you, perhaps they are trying to achieve something positive in their own way. Maybe they think that it makes them appear stronger in front of others? Or it will teach you a good lesson? Sometimes it's hard to fathom out what the positive intention could be, and yet it's usually possible to come up with one. This suggests that the other person is trying, in some strange way, to be helpful either to you, to help others or to help themselves? Whatever the reason, try to take it positively, appreciate it, and move on.

To summarise, try to identify your own purpose(s) and write it/them down on a piece of paper. Try to ensure that it is something positive that you really think is aligned to you and your own beliefs and identity, and then try to be proactive about achieving it.

Remind yourself of your purpose often, and try to take one step towards it each and every day. You may want to write a one-line summary of it, and keep it visible so that you see it every day. Just looking at it once every day could have a profound effect.

P

Key Points

➢ Think about your own purpose, what you want to achieve, write it down, focus on it.

➢ Remember that the things you've done in the past, or are doing now, will help you in the future.

➢ If you notice something that isn't right or that you could help with, then say something, or do something about it.

➢ Always look at situations positively and learn something from them.

➢ Be proactive and make things happen.

O

Objectives

Opportunities

Outcome focussed

Oh, so here we are at the next letter of the **POINT** acronym. The "O" stands for Outcome. You can change it to a word of your choice of course, this is not carved in stone, but Outcome seemed to be right in my mind.

What do you want your Outcome or Outcomes to be?

What are your main aims and Objectives?

Alongside this, are you looking out for opportunities?

What do you want to achieve? Is it something really tangible and can you measure it? Perhaps it is to get an A in Maths, a B in Biology, to be able to run the 400 metres in under 60 seconds, or swim a mile? Or perhaps it is to play a song on the guitar, give a presentation or reach a certain level in dance? Not all at the same time though! Your aims and objectives will change over time, and it is worth considering what you would like to try to achieve in say, 6 months' time, or one year, or perhaps three years?

Have a go at writing some down, and see how you get on. You can change them, remove them, and add new ones at any time, because they are yours.

Whatever you want to achieve, it is personal to you, and everyone has something they want to achieve, something that will make them happy. Often we are trying to please others, our parents, friends, peers, siblings, and this is fine. Alongside this, make sure you have objectives for YOU, and you alone...as these will see you through, along your own personal journey in life.

Could you write some down now?

The mere act of writing them on a piece of paper could help you shape them and help you to realise what they are, and build on them. Do you have friends who have achieved something that you would like to achieve?

It's really good to have a direction to move towards and setting realistic Objectives can often help. Try to make each of them positive and forward looking. Typically if you do more things that make you happy, then the bad stuff, or problem areas in your life should sort themselves out.

Bear in mind that if you start a new behavior and do it regularly, daily for 20 days for example, it will become a habit and your mind will start to regard it as normal behavior and so bear with it, for it will become easier in time.

Here are a few examples based on some typical "problem areas" and potential objectives:

- If you think that you lack confidence:
  - Enrol onto a drama group
  - Talk to someone new every week
  - Read a book about confidence
  - Prepare a short presentation about something you enjoy and deliver it to your family
  - Ask someone who is confident how they do it

- If you think that you are overweight:
  - Start doing the Parkrun every week
  - Try to eat at least three pieces of fruit every day
  - Try to do some form of exercise every day
  - Walk or cycle to school/work
  - When you feel a craving for a snack, try drinking a glass of water instead

- If you have concerns about your body image:
  - Eat healthily
  - Exercise more
  - Volunteer at an old people's home
  - Stop taking selfies

- If you think that you get stressed too much:
  - Try to meditate for 5 minutes every day
  - Start to write a diary entry every day
  - Read a book about overcoming stress
  - Exercise 20 minutes every day and take a bath on Sunday

- If you think that you are being bullied

- o   Enrol onto a self-defence course
- o   Talk to someone about it
- o   Ask the person why they are bullying you
- o   Decide to stand up to it and push back (bullies are usually cowards)

- If you think that you are depressed:
  - o   Talk to your parents and friends
  - o   Start doing more exercise
  - o   Talk to your doctor
  - o   Learn to meditate or practice mindfulness

- If you want to stop smoking
  - o   Try to write down 5 good reasons to stop
  - o   Try to have a smoke free day today (and try again tomorrow)
  - o   Save the money you would have spent on cigarettes and buy something else you desire

Of course when you are defining objectives you should try to make sure that each one is **SMART** - Clearly stated (**S**pecific), you know whether you have definitely achieved it or not (**M**easurable), it is possible (**A**chievable), it is in line with your aims and purpose (**R**elevant) and has a date or time limit (**T**imely).

The main thing is that you are happy with your objectives, as you are the one who is going to do them, and so if you can add two more letters to SMART to make it **SMARTIE**. The "I" stands for Interesting and the "E" stands for Enjoyable. Yes, if your objectives are in line with the SMARTIE acronym then that's sure to make you Smile, so you can now add the "S" and it becomes **SMARTIES**…and everyone loves those!

As an alternative way to look at things, a bit of reverse psychology if you like, let us try to consider how someone else might look at things. Instead of trying to make the most of life, this next section takes a reverse look at what it takes to be a complete flop. It is intended to help you to understand that, no matter how you may currently feel, you can make your life better by focusing on the right things.

How to be a complete flop

Don't decide what you want. If you do decide on what you want, don't think about why you want it. And if you do decide why you want it, commit to believing that you can't have it.

The worst thing you can do, if you are truly committed to being one of life's flops, is to decide what you want. It has been proven, in study after study, that people who have vision, goals, self belief and a real sense of purpose in what they do, are the most successful and fulfilled individuals on the planet.

Success is all about luck. Ask any failure and that is what they'll say. Someone once said that success was simply a decision – and the decision was around what you want to be, do and have. In that moment of decision you become a successful person. So don't do it!

As children we dream about what we could achieve. My advice is don't think about what your dream is or was. Don't imagine that it's still possible to still live it. Don't be an ambitious dreamer. Just carry on and do what you've always done, as this is perhaps the best way of wasting years of your life.

In a survey they asked people who had reached the age of 100 what they had most regretted, and they said they had wished they had taken more risks and done more of the things that made them happy. If you want to be able to say the same thing when you are 100, then don't focus on what you want.

Keep thinking about what you don't want!

Now that we're on a new page, coming back to reality again, **think about what you do want!**

Every great achievement starts with a small step in the right direction. Try to make just one small step towards what you might like to do. What's the harm? It's low risk because you can at any time decide to stop and try something else. Who knows, you might enjoy it, learn something and decide to make another step. That first step could be profound and could well be the best thing that you have ever done. What could you do today?

Stephen Covey wrote a book called "*Seven habits of highly effective people*" and one of these habits is "Begin with the end in mind". I think that this is very important to consider when doing most things in life. If you are about to start doing something, where do you want to get to at the end? What does the end look like, feel like or sound like?

I wrote a song about his seven habits so if you're looking for some light relief and catchy choruses that will help you to remember all seven habits, then check out my "Synergize Song" on YouTube, which can be found here: https://www.youtube.com/watch?v=bo1h8Sn0-Z8. Currently it has only been viewed 7 times (strangely enough in line with the 7 habits), so please help to increase that number. Getting into double figures would be good. This song is not to be taken too seriously, it was just a spot of light relief at the time.

Something else to consider is that, although it's really important to have an outcome to work towards and a specific achievement to reach, the main activity is the journey that you take to get there. Yes you can enjoy the fact that you have achieved an objective, and this is a great feeling. You have completed something of value, and usually, when you think about it, the journey that you took to get there was amazing in its own right. It's great to have an end to journey towards, but it's the journey that matters in the end. This is so true, and so embrace each journey.

Opportunities often come along in life and if you are prepared and ready for them, then you will be able to take advantage of them. If you want to be an Astronaut then you will need to have excellent academic qualifications, learn how to fly planes, be extremely fit and be ready for the unlikely possibility that an opportunity might arise for you to go into space.

It is very unlikely that a person would end up going into space, but it happens. People do, and in order for them to be in a position to do so, they must be prepared for it, which is likely to mean years and years of focused hard work and determination. Just ask Chris Hadfield, who was the first Canadian astronaut to walk in space. As a child he watched the Apollo 11 Moon landing on TV and from that point onwards he knew what his dream was, and aged 33 he was selected to go into space. His dream had come true. Most of us have easier dreams, and so ours are a lot more likely to come true!

Some people have a fear of failure. They are worried that if they embark on something and do not achieve it then they will feel a failure. I think that this is an irrational fear in today's world for most of us. I think that fear is a natural feeling that is part of our evolutionary DNA and has helped us to survive over millions of years, as we perceive something as a dangerous threat.

For example if, say 2 million years ago, a stone age family decided to leave their cave and walk into the jungle without any weapons they might all get eaten alive! Or perhaps they decide to look after a pet snake and try to make the Black Mamba feel at home. That probably wouldn't turn out particularly well. Fear of danger has kept us safe over thousands of years.

These days our levels of fear are pretty low, however our brains still have this fundamental function of feeling fear, getting stressed, anxious and worried and really it is mostly completely overkill. We all experience it to some degree, and we each deal with it differently. It is our unconscious mind trying to be helpful, to guide us to avoid pain and death.

If the thing that you're fearing is not dangerous, or you accept the risks, then feel the fear, accept it, understand that it is part of who you are, then move on and do it anyway! Usually you will not die.

If you want to do something that is physically achievable, and is not likely to be harmful to yourself or anyone else, then do it, because if you don't then, and only then, have you failed.

Imagine when you first started to walk if you hadn't taken that first step because you were afraid that you might not be able to do it. You tried, probably fell over and tried again, and this probably went on for weeks and then one day, you managed to walk a few steps...you were walking! This is all part of the process of learning.

Think about it, if someone else can do something then you probably can as well. So if you see someone else doing something that you'd like to do, give it a go!

When you think back over your life and recall the best memories you have, they were probably when you did something a little bit scary, perhaps you were outside of your comfort zone or tried really hard at achieving something and did it! Quite rightly you will have ignored the many times you "failed". In fact there really is no "failure" because each time you "fail" you learn something and you only really fail when you stop trying…so just keep trying, you will get there in the end.

Consider adjusting your aims slightly. That might be what is required in order for you to achieve it, or break it down into more manageable chunks and just try to achieve the next small step. Every big change starts with a small step.

Some people choose to procrastinate, and put things off, and I would say just try to make a start on whatever it is that you want to work towards. Decide now an approach and you have a 50% chance that it's right, so go ahead. Once you start you can then review it in a few days or weeks' time and, like a ship sailing towards land, adjust your course from time to time, to keep going towards what you want.

Objectives can be small, very small. If you want to start doing exercise then you could start by doing just 1 minute a day. You could jog on the spot before brushing your teeth, or perhaps do 5 push-ups every morning? If you want to write a book, you could commit to writing at least one sentence every day? Then, if you want to, you can change the Objective when you feel like it. They are your objectives that you are setting for yourself, and the person benefiting from them is you, so they should evolve as you do and as your mood changes.

If you want to reduce your weight and tone your body up, then take each day at a time and try to do something positive towards your goal each day, no matter how small, it is still a step forward. There is no need to think too far into the future.

It can be good to have specific targets in the future such as I have just this month enrolled in a 5K Open Water Swim in six months' time. I've never swam more than 1.5K in one go, and that was in an indoor swimming pool. I've bought a second hand wetsuit and I plan to start swimming outside in one month's time, and what I hope to do is to take each swim, day, week at a time and see how it progresses.

I will try to swim a bit further each time I go to the lake, and hopefully in six months time, I will be able to complete the 5K distance. Either way, my swimming is bound to have improved and I should be a lot fitter, and so I will still have benefited.

If you smoke or take any drugs, try to give them up for today. Just today. Don't think about tomorrow as you can choose tomorrow morning what you're going to do tomorrow. Just focus on today and try not to smoke today, or whatever it is that you don't want to do. Decide in the morning that just for today you will not do it. If you do end up relenting and for example smoke a cigarette, then that's fine, you can always try not to again tomorrow. Keep trying and just for today. Before long you will see that the urge to repeat the habit is diminishing.

The same approach can work with diets, just try to eat a bit less or healthier food today, and then tomorrow you can choose whether you try again for another day, or change the diet, or try something new. Each day, try to do something for yourself.

By now you should be starting to believe that you could change your life. You could stop doing the things that you don't want to do, and start doing more of the things that you do want to do. You could do it, and you could start now.

O

Key Points

➤ Focus on your desired outcome and get closer to it one step at a time.

➤ Look out for opportunities and be ready to embrace them.

➤ Remember, it's better to try than not to try.

➤ Do more of what you love.

I

Interests

Be Interested

What's Important to you?

Interests are very important. What are you interested in? TV? Computer Games? Sport? Science? Fast cars? Making Money? Eating? People? Magic? Collecting postcards?

Everyone is interested in something, what are you interested in? What do you identify with?

When you consider what you are interested in, and what "makes you tick" this can really help you in relation to establishing your own Purpose and Outcomes. So think back to the P and the O and hopefully some of this will be linking together now, and aligning. The "P" the "O" and the "I" should all be related to some degree, even if this is in very small amounts.

Choose your attitude – if you are curious and interested in what's going on, you will start to notice more, and things will become more interesting for you.

We filter so much of what is going on and we miss so much. Have you ever noticed that if you think about something, like a particular car, then you tend to see the same make or model on the road quite often?

It's almost as if they stand out. You could try it today, look for people wearing hats. You are likely to see a lot more than you normally would (especially if it's winter!) and this is because for most of the time you do see them but they are not significant and so your brain ignores them, as it does with almost everything you see. Try looking for people wearing red…how many can you see today?

Your brain is amazing. It is constantly receiving vast amounts of information through your eyes with light hitting the back of your retina and being transformed and interpreted in certain ways, and peripheral vision monitoring movement all around you.

Your ears are listening for sounds and are able to identify the precise location of the sound with amazing accuracy, as a result of the tiny difference in sound arrival at each ear. You have an excellent sense of smell and taste, and can feel movements and temperature changes.

Basically, there is a lot going on, and your brain has to try to make some sense of it all, and, similar to a newspaper it has to ignore a lot of what is happening and focus on the headlines. If a particular subject is being focused on in the news, such as a political event, then a newspaper will focus on that (often exaggerating and simplifying it at the same time) and defocus the rest. Your brain does a similar thing, although hopefully it is focusing on headlines that are not made up.

We, you and me, all human beings are unconscious.

Yes that is true, we are unconscious beings. It may sound a bit weird, but it's true. Most of what we do is completely unconscious. The way our heart beats, the way we digest food, our dreams, and the way we quickly remove our hand from a hot plate are all completely unconscious actions.

Wait a moment! You might be thinking, we are also conscious beings, and I agree with you, yes we are. We are also conscious, and I would suggest that our level of consciousness is perhaps similar to an iceberg with the top part sticking out of the water being our conscious awareness, and the major part, lurking under the waterline is our unconscious part.

Your mind is a bit like the RAM memory in a computer, it is actively aware of what is happening and is able to store a few things at the same time about what is happening now, perhaps three or four things, which can then be processed by your brain.

In addition to this there is a lot more storage space in the background capable of holding and processing information that you are not actually aware of. There are patterns of behavior, and habits that we have learnt and that have been passed through to our unconscious mind, and we are likely to repeat these patterns of behavior until we consciously try to change them.

We are able to learn things such as walking, running and talking and after a while of trying to do these things in a conscious way by actually thinking hard to do them, these routines become unconscious. Some things like breathing and walking we can do consciously and unconsciously, so we effectively share the control, up to a point.

Be aware that the unconscious mind is stronger though. It's nice to think that we are in control of ourselves, and in a way we are, because our conscious and unconscious are both parts of our own mind. We can consciously take control of our breathing and hold our breath for a few minutes, but after a while our unconscious mind helpfully forces us to take another breath. They both work together for our own benefit.

Not only is our unconscious part of our brain stronger, it is also a lot quicker, this is apparent when something unexpected happens such as when we pick up an object that is hot and immediately release it, or when we duck at a loud noise and our heart starts to beat faster, so that we can fight, freeze or flight.

We are apes. We are the most advanced beings in the world, top of the food chain, and have an understanding and awareness of what and who we are, but don't be fooled into thinking that we know it all. We don't. We have a limited understanding of our capabilities, and ourselves, and yet there is so much more that we don't understand.

We are amazing creatures and there is a lot going on underneath the scenes that is keeping us alive and helping us grow and progress in life. When I was a kid at school, I used to have a badge that I quite liked that had the following statement on it: "*If the human brain was simple enough for us to understand, we'd be too simple to understand it*". I liked the simple paradoxical logic to this statement and thought it was worthy of buying and wearing, which I did for a few days, until I lost it.

I like to think that the way we work is similar to a car. We take the steering wheel and are able to drive a car with the accelerator and brake, and drive in a certain way. We can steer the car and drive it slowly, fast, efficiently or erratically. We are in control and we can choose how effective we are, and also how we react when things happen. Do you slow down for the bumps in the road, avoid the potholes and make efficient progress?

We can choose how we drive it, but we are unlikely to have anything to do with how the engine works, the gears interlink, or how the wheels actually turn. This is all happening under the bonnet and we don't really care. As cars get more advanced they now include features such as Collision protection when the car applies the brakes on our behalf, or parking sensors that can sense if we're too close. We are mainly in control when we're driving, well, at least we think we are.

Our bodies have similar hidden features that are active and monitoring things happening all around us. Accepting this can be very enlightening and can help give more understanding to feelings of intuition or why you might have Goosebumps or feel uncomfortable in someone's presence...your unconscious senses are telling you something about the situation or the other person. You are not consciously aware of it, but your unconscious is, and it's often worth listening to.

Everybody needs to have some time out now and again, and for most people this is done as part of a hobby. Doing something fun, interesting and which involves some kind of learning is really good for you. Some people enjoy spending time on a pastime such as jogging or playing chess, drawing or playing a guitar etc. These are often things that they have been introduced to, but there are a lot of people who have never even considered a past time. Or people who perhaps think it is a waste of time.

Hobbies are really important as an outlet. It gives you something else to focus on from time to time and take your mind away from other more mundane things. Focusing on a hobby has the wonderful advantage of pushing any nagging concerns out of your mind for a while.

Having a hobby can reduce or eliminate any anxiety you might have and seriously improve sleep at night. So try if you can to think of one for yourself. Ideally something physical, practical, or creative like playing an instrument – whatever it is, try to find something that you truly enjoy doing and something that you can still see yourself doing in years to come. Of course hobbies will come and go, but some of them will stay with you throughout your life, like a trusted friend; a place to go when you need to get away.

Imagine yourself in ten years' time as an expert in some pastime – what would it be? Why not give it a go and try it? No harm in trying one out and if it's no good for you, try another; until you find something you look forward to doing.

As I sit here writing this book, on 14th March 2018, I hear on the news that the visionary British Physicist and author Stephen Hawking has died. He was an amazing person who, despite having a rare motor neurone disease, which left him paralysed, he managed to perform amazing scientific work from his wheelchair. Somehow, despite not being able to walk, talk, or move any of his body apart from, towards the end, a single cheek muscle, he used his mind for ground-breaking theories around black holes and cosmology.

I feel humbled thinking about what he achieved with apparently so little, and how he coped with not being able to move. If he was able to do so much in his situation, then I am so fortunate, and I find it really inspirational. It just shows that we can all do so much in the world if we try.

He delivered a number of memorable quotes, and one of my favourites is this one:

"Remember to look up at the stars and not down at your feet. Try to make sense of what you see and wonder about what makes the universe exist. Be curious. And however difficult life may seem, there is always something you can do and succeed at. It matters that you don't just give up."

Try to find something that interests you, and is important to you, and enjoy it.

Consider what is really important to you. So often we fill our day-to-day lives with things that we feel we have to do, and urgent matters that need attention. Life is busy, we need to keep in contact with people, read emails, work, entertain, clean the house, wash the car, exercise, catch-up on social media, watch TV, tidy the house etc. Accept that you do actually have a lot of choice and question whether you really do need to do all of these things. So often people focus on what is urgent, and sometimes neglect the things that are important.

Remember to think about what is really important in your life, perhaps it is about family or a specific relationship that you have, realise that it is important, and make sure you make time for it and foster it. It is often only when things fall apart that people realise what was really important.

I find that when I go away, especially on my own, that I soon realise what I am missing the most, and what is really important to me. I really miss the things that I love and care about, and I can assure you that it is not the emails!

When you spend time on the important things in life, you will notice that the other less important things may not get done – this is fine. You cannot and will not get everything done, nobody ever has and nobody ever will. If you are able to focus on the most important 20%, then you should find that this results in 80% satisfaction. Invest your time and energy in the key important things is the key to happiness. This is in line with the Pareto principle, which states that 80% of the effect comes from 20% of the causes.

Focus on the key important aspects of your life and the rest will fall into line.

I

Key Points

➢ Accept that you are only partly conscious – be true to yourself and trust that your unconscious mind will support you and work with you.

➢ Understand that you filter most of what's going on

➢ Focus on what is important.

➢ Embrace your interests, enjoy them and take pleasure from them.

N

Notice

Be Nice

New behaviours

Notice what you do and how you do it. We all act differently and we each typically have habitual ways of approaching things, dealing with issues and responding to events.

It is worth sometimes noticing how you operate, taking a step back and considering what you have done today. How you have done it compared to how others would have done it, or how they did it?

All of us see, hear and feel things differently and we each behave in our own way based on our knowledge, skills, beliefs and values. I'd like to state that again because it really is quite profound: All of us see, hear and feel things differently.

We process all of the information that we receive through our own senses and we each hear something slightly different, see something slightly different and feel something different. When all of our senses combine, including smell and taste, the information we take varies massively from person to person.

Each of us filters, generalizes and distorts the information that we receive in order for it to make sense, because basically there is too much information. We then process the information and we may then make a judgment, or react in a certain way.

Accepting that we all experience something different can be helpful to understand why people behave differently. I have no proof to back up what I am about to say and in fact it's just my own theory, but I think that the reason that some people appear to have more colour co-ordination than others could be because we all see colours differently. Some people say that, for clothing combinations *"Blue and green should never be seen, unless there's something in-between"*. What if you see the colour green as others see gray (which is meant to go well with blue)? To you. and many others, it will look great.

Nobody knows how anyone else sees any colours because we interpret them ourselves based on their electromagnetic wavelength. It's a bit like us each having our own unique map of the world and no two are the same. They may be similar, but no two are exactly the same. It's bizarre to think that nothing ever really happened as you remember it, because your senses will have distorted parts of it, and that we all sense and think differently.

Do you think that what you did yesterday or today was good? Was it the only way? Could you have done it differently? If there is someone whom you aspire to be like, how would they have done the things that you did? Would they have done them in the same way do you think?

If you think that you might be able to improve how you approach or deliver something, notice what you could consider changing and then next time, try the new behaviour. If you think it has helped, and resulted in a better outcome, well done, keep at it. If it hasn't helped then try something else, or go back to what you were doing.

It's worth noticing that when you behave differently, other people react differently too. You can influence change all around you. Try it and you will see.

Have you ever tried to stop and just be in the moment?

All you have to do is nothing.

You could try it now.

Sounds simple right? Well, it is.

Just try not to think about anything. It's simple but also quite hard to do. Perhaps try it properly after reading this paragraph. Try to be truly present, in the moment. Relax, breathe slowly and deeply, and clear your mind.

In fact, your mind is very active and it is continuously focusing on what's going in. There is so much happening at any point in time that your brain is continually scanning the environment for things to hear, see, smell, taste, feel and in our busy worlds there is often a lot of noise and activity competing for our attention.

It's only possible to hold a few things in our mind at the same time, and so if you try to focus hard on your own breathing, then this helps to push other stuff out of your mind. With more practice it gets easier and if you try to do it every day then over the next few days and weeks you will find it becomes easier and is rather enjoyable.

If you want to give it a go, just for a few minutes, try these three simple steps:

1) Sit comfortably with your eyes gently closed.

2) Try to listen to, and think about your own breathing.

3) When thoughts come into your mind, try to focus back on your breath again.

When you face a problem, what happens? How do you deal with it? Are you someone who deals with things effectively? Do you ever wonder how other people seem to deal with things in a different way to you? Perhaps they are more effective in dealing with problems that come along, or perhaps the simple things seem to overwhelm them.

Whatever other people do, and whatever you do, accept that you handle things better than some people and also less effectively that other people.

Some people refer to a problem as being a *"Monkey"* that needs managing. Ideally, according to the *"Golden rules"*, monkeys should either be fed or shot. If instead they starve to death, then valuable time is wasted in conducting post-mortems.

So, if a monkey comes your way, try to either feed it and pass it onto someone else or shoot it. Try not to let the monkey sit on your back because before too long you will have several of them, and it will feel overwhelming. Take action whenever possible and move it forward. Deal with it and move on, ideally and fairly passing the next action onto someone else.

The other thing about "noticing" is to listen and really listen. Do you listen effectively? We hear noises and sounds, and hear other people talking, but quite often people just hear the words, interpret them and then start thinking about their own reply, and don't focus on what the other person or people are really saying. Do you do this?

When you are talking to someone else, how nice is it when that person is fully engaged with you, really actively listening to your words and to the message that you are trying to convey to them.

It is nice to be listened to; it feels good. It is respectful and is appreciated, and so try hard to offer the same back to the other person. Listen effectively and intently to what they are saying, and if you can, actively listen on three levels as follows:

1. Listen to the <u>words</u> that they are saying with your **head** and try hard to understand what they are describing.

2. Listen to the <u>feelings</u> that they are also communicating with the message with your **heart**.

3. Listen to the <u>meaning</u> of the communication with your **gut**. What is the real meaning of the communication?

Try to consider these three levels of listening during your next conversation(s) and alongside this, give the other person an opportunity to speak and tell you all that they want to say. It's good to respond with small encouraging words such as "Yes" or "I see", "quite" etc. and with nods of the head etc. and try hard not to reply too quickly or finish of their sentence for them.

Listening at these three separate levels is hard, and yet with practice it becomes easier and your unconscious mind will automatically start to adopt this new behaviour in time.

You have two ears and one mouth and some people say that you should use them in the same proportion i.e. listen to twice the amount that you speak, and I agree with this philosophy. You know what you think, and so it's usually much more beneficial to listen to the other person's message, and really trying to understand it from their point of view.

Once you understand fully what they are saying, and their views, you can then explain your thoughts, and try, if possible, to find something that you both agree on. Something that you both think is right and then take it from there. Trying to agree on a step forward that you are both happy with.

Reflect on where you are now, take a step back and try to look at your life from an external perspective. Imagine looking through the window of your house and looking at yourself. What things would you like to change about yourself, things that you would like to start doing more of, or things that you would like to achieve?

What are you currently spending a lot of your time doing? Is it aligned to what you want to be? If not, then it's time to do something about it. Decide and take action. Today would be the best time to start.

Do you have friends or colleagues who you respect and who seem to live life well and appear to be confident and happy most of the time? If so, consider asking them how they like to live their lives. How do they face the challenges of life? Do they have a specific approach? How does it feel? What's important to them?

You might be able to learn from these people and consider trying something different yourself. Ask for feedback, how do they think you're doing? Ask them to give you some feedback on what they think you could do better. Receive any feedback as a gift and then consider it. If you agree that it makes sense then take it on board and if you think that it does not make sense or is not relevant, then ignore it. Notice what is going on.

Do you notice your own habits? We all have habits that we perform routinely, and many of them we don't even realize we're doing. Some are good and some are bad. We often do the same things on a daily basis such as: Getting up at a certain time, performing bathroom duties in a certain order, eating the same breakfast, watching the same TV programs or listening to the same radio station at the same time every day.

Being creatures of habit helps us to cope with the many activities that we need to perform on a daily basis, and the way that this works is that when we repeat certain tasks, our mind recognises a pattern and then tries to simplify it by learning the repetition and then moving the process into the unconscious part of the mind. This way we can then get on and learn other things. The trouble is that sometimes we learn bad habits or just become "stuck in our ways".

I enjoy swimming and meet up with a triathlon training team every week, and although I am a relatively good swimmer (able to swim 400 metre freestyle in around 8.5 minutes), I am one of the slower ones in the group. I try hard to swim faster, but have been struggling to make any improvements. So, a few weeks ago I went to a swimming coach and was filmed swimming from above and also underwater both from the side and also from the front.

Afterwards, whilst viewing and analysing my stroke with the coach, it was apparent that my arms were crossing over the centre line causing my body to go out of alignment resulting in me "snaking" through the water, which was slowing me down. What I need to do is to imaging my hand and arm entry is at the same position as 10 AM and 2 PM on a clock face. So instead of putting my hands up towards midday, I have to put them out towards the sides of the pool more.

I have tried this since and it feels really weird, it feels like I am putting my arms out too far to the side, however in reality they are going straight ahead. This seems to relate to the fact that my body is turning in the water and so although it feels like my hands are entering the water at the wrong angle, they are in fact aligned forward correctly. Basically I have learnt this inefficient way of swimming over many years by repeating the same action and it being re-enforced in my unconscious mind.

It also seems that when I take a breath to one side or the other, the other arm doesn't pull effectively. Instead of pulling the water back, I seem to be pushing the water down. According to the coach, this is something I probably learnt when I first started swimming (around 40 years ago!) because it kept my head above water, and I'm still doing it.

If I can learn to change this behavior, which I will, I will swim a lot faster and more efficiently. It's hard to change, but important to do so if I want to get faster. I now need to consciously put effort in to change my technique until it becomes unconscious.

People say "*Practice makes Perfect*", and I think this is a good saying with a good message. However, according to Mike, a friend of mine, a more realistic version is *"Practice makes Permanent"*, and I agree with him. Up to a point anyway, because the thing to remember is that it is not permanent. Basically, whatever you practice gets re-enforced, whether it's good or bad. If it is a learnt behavior then you can change it and learn a better way. I will keep working on my swimming technique and then that will become permanent until it changes again in the future! I can actively break this inefficient habit by consciously forcing myself to behave differently, and in time this will be my new more efficient habit.

So, I think that a better saying could be *"Practice makes Permanent... for now"*.

To sum up, it is worth thinking about what things you do on a regular basis, notice what's happening, and asking yourself whether there is another way to approach it. Usually there are many ways and it might be worth trying to do something different for a change. Try another way, and if it doesn't make an improvement, then either go back to what you were doing before or try yet another way.

If you do what you've always done, you'll get what you've always got, so think about trying something new, and after a while that will become your new behavior. You could try to get up 15 minutes earlier and do some stretching every morning, or listen to a different radio channel or move the TV to another position in the room, or listen to music instead of watching the TV, or do your homework straight after school, or do it later in the evening? Just try something different and see how it feels and what the results are.

If you are starting a new habit try to think of a small reward that you will give yourself, such as a smoothie after a run, or just stand in front of the mirror and say "Well done" to yourself. That may sound a bit weird, but it really can be effective, because it really helps to have a positive message afterwards...perhaps play one of your favourite songs loud, or spend 10 minutes on your favourite hobby?

Different people do things in different ways and at different times and so ask your friends what routines they have that they think are beneficial to them, and perhaps try some of them on for size? You might enjoy the change or become enlightened to their ways?

All of our routines were created in the past and you can change them now and in the future. Your past makes you what you are today, don't make it your burden. You can choose today to try something different and change your future to be what you want it to be.

Another thing to notice is that we all have bad days from time to time and sometimes they are related to our actions and sometimes nothing to do with our actions at all. Stuff happens and there are some things that we have to deal with when things don't quite work out how we'd hoped. All I can say on this subject is that what's done is done, and if you can try to remove the emotion away from the event then that is a good thing.

It's quite hard to do so sometimes, and yet doing this can really help you to find an objective way forward and to try to move on. The best way to deal with something that you don't like is to focus on a positive outcome and move towards the result that you want. Consider how best to move on and try to identify a goal to work towards, and then take a step towards it. Bad times and sad times will pass, so try to move to pastures new and see the blue sky above the rain.

I like to watch how people react to things and how some people always seem to see the positives in life and how some people see the negatives. Also how some people are trying to move forward towards something that they want, and others try to get away from something they don't want. I find it fascinating and I encourage you to try watching the people around you and see if you can spot their behavioural habits. It can be very interesting, especially when you then start wondering what your own behavioural habits are, and whether they are in line with what you want them to be. Do you think you have good behaviours?

I love puzzles and there is an interesting probability puzzle that I heard once and I find it fascinating to watch how people react to it. Of course if they know it already then the reaction is not that spectacular, but if it is new to them, the response that you might see is quite remarkable. The puzzle is about three boxes, one of which has a prize inside it, and the others are empty, it goes like this:

There are three boxes, let's call them Box A, Box B and Box C. Inside one of the boxes is a prize, and the other two boxes are empty. The thing is, you don't know which box has the prize, and you have to select one. Whichever one you select at this point doesn't make any difference, because each one has an equal chance (1 in 3) of being the box with the prize in it. So you can select box A, box B or box C it makes no difference. So now in your own mind, please select a box: A, B or C.

Have you selected one?

Okay, so once you have selected a box I will take one of the other two boxes and open it to reveal that there is nothing inside. So for example, if you selected box A, then I will either open box B or box C and reveal that it's empty.

Now what remains are two boxes, the one that you originally selected, and the other remaining box.

You still don't know which box contains the prize, and you now have a choice. You can either stick with the box that you first selected, or you can swap your selection to be the other box. The question to this puzzle is what do you do and why. I see there being three approaches as follows:

1. Stick with the first box selected because it's more likely to contain the prize.

2. Swap to the other box because it's more likely to contain the prize.

3. It makes no difference; they both have the same chance of containing the prize.

What do you think is the right option? Stick, swap or it makes no difference?

Given this scenario, what would you do?

I will reveal the answer in due course. It is a fascinating puzzle because most people will come up with the wrong answer, and often, when they do, many people will dispute it when the answer is revealed. Some people will be in denial for quite a while, and may never accept it. You might do the same, and in fact when I first heard the puzzle I got the answer wrong.

When I first heard this puzzle, I thought about it for a while and then decided that, as far as I was concerned it made no difference whatsoever, and so in my mind the option was definitely Option 3. The prize could be in either box and that each one had a 50% chance of containing the prize.

Then when I looked at the answer I saw that it was option 2, swap to the other box! Apparently it was more probably that the prize was in the other box. I did not understand how swapping to the other box could increase my chance of winning the prize, and also it felt uncomfortable swapping the box because I felt that in a strange way I had an allegiance to the original box selected. So I was sure that sticking with my first selection was best, although I thought that both boxes had the same chance.

I thought it was an interesting puzzle and it remained in my mind as I went to bed.

The next morning my opinion changed. It was strange really because when I woke up, I had this image of there being a whole pack of 52 cards laying in a line on the floor. All of these cards were originally face down and I had been asked to select the Ace of Spades. I had selected one card (which had a 2% chance of being the Ace of Spades) and all of the other cards had been turned over one at a time, leaving just one other card towards the end of the line. The person turning over the cards knew where the Ace of Spades was and if it was in the 51 cards not selected, it would be left face down. Now, in this situation would you still stick with your selected card, or would you swap to the other one that has been left face-down?

It appeared to me that somehow, overnight, my unconscious mind had thought about the problem, exaggerated the concept, come up with another example and then presented it to me the following morning. And it then made a lot more sense and I accepted that swapping is the best option.

When you make you first selection then the % probability remains, so in the case of the three boxes when you first made a selection, there was a 33% chance of it being correct, and so the remaining 67% was with the other two boxes. When one of the two boxes was shown to be empty, the 67% was left wholly with the "other" box. In the case of the playing cards, your originally selected card would still have a 2% chance of being the Ace of Spades, and the other card would have a 98% chance. You may still have chosen the correct card, but it's unlikely. It has a 1 in 52 chance of being correct.

I hope you found this puzzle interesting and if you don't agree that you have more chance of winning if you swap, then try thinking about it overnight and let your unconscious mind help you understand it. Alternatively try it with a pack of cards.

As I said beforehand, the main interesting thing about this puzzle is that when you explain it to someone and actually give them the answer, quite often they will not agree with you. They will not accept it and may disagree quite strongly, in fact I have had people argue about it for about an hour and get quite cross about it, and it's fascinating to watch their behavior. Then, at some point they will get it. It might be in a few minutes, a few hours or a few days, but they will get it in the end, usually!

To me this highlights how we believe what we want to believe. We think something makes sense and so we choose to believe it, and it's hard to be swayed from this opinion. Some people believe in Christianity, some people are Hindu, some are Islamic, some are Sikhs, some are Buddhists, some don't believe in a religion, and to each one of us we believe what we believe, because, usually, that is what we have been brought up to believe. That is what we have been told is the truth. When you think about it, it's likely that only one of these could possibly be right, and so most of them are likely to be wrong. Trying to suggest that someone changes from one religion to another is likely to be problematic most of the time, and so I'd suggest it's best not to try, but isn't it fascinating what different people believe in, and often they never even question it.

In the case of the three box puzzle, try explaining it to someone and watch what they do. If they say to you that it makes no difference and then you explain that if they swap the box then they double their chances of winning, watch their reaction and see how easily or hard they are able to adjust to a new belief. It really is fascinating and can help you see how difficult change can be for some people. It's worth noticing and watching how some people struggle with new ideas and new behaviours. Learning to be more flexible, listening to reason and adapting to change can help you grow.

Try to do one thing nice each day. The more people do nice things, the nicer the world becomes. It makes other people happier and it also makes you a more worthwhile person.

N

Key Points

➤ Look around – watch others – learn from them.

➤ Be in the moment, here and now.

➤ Listen with your head, heart and gut.

➤ Be receptive to change and try learning new behaviours.

➤ Be nice.

T

Try

Today

The flaws add value

Try to see the blue sky above the clouds. However grey the sky is, the blue sky will come eventually, and when it's really dark you can see the stars shine.

The focus here is to try, every day, just try!

You, yes you dear reader, are a wonderful creature. You have evolved over millions of years of continuous, successful survival and reproduction. During this incredibly unlikely and unbroken line of development, you have become stronger, more resilient, more adaptable, more intelligent and longer living than your ancestors. You are the most up to date version.

It is incredible that you are here at all, especially when you consider that apparently over 99% of species that have existed on Earth are now extinct. You are a survivor and you are a winner in the battle of natural selection and survival of the fittest.

One of the main concepts of natural selection is the constant struggle for survival, which is a test of the species and results in the stronger or more adaptable ones surviving, who then pass on their genes to the next generation. The weaker ones die out.

Life is hard sometimes, and everyone will have his or her battles to fight. You might be going through a battle right now, or you have done in the past, or you will in the future. Whatever it is, and whenever it is, so often it is at these "dark" times that the stars shine, and if you can hold your resolve and focus on moving forward, you will shine brighter! When it's dark you can see the stars.

Some people want to do something but are afraid of trying. This is very common and quite understandable. Failure is not nice. I once tried to balance my swim bag on the top of the front wheel of my bicycle and it fell to the side got jammed in the wheel, and I got flung over the handle bars and landed on the ground. It was very painful and I felt like an idiot and never did it again. It did highlight to me that we learn a lot from our failures, probably a lot more than we learn from our successes, and often the more painful it is, the stronger the learning.

When on holiday in the Maldives, I swam out a long way from the island and when I turned to swim back, I became caught in a rip current that was determined to take me out further to sea. It was a very scary moment for me and somehow I managed to get back to the safety of the beach. I really had to fight against the force of the water, and that day I learnt a valuable lesson, and won't swim out that far again in a hurry.

There are other things that I have done that I have successfully completed, such as the London Marathon, which, I am really pleased that I did. I could have failed, but I didn't, and in my opinion, if there is something that you want to do and you are worried about failing, that is fine, just try. If you decide not to try, then you have already failed.

I was on a leadership training course one day, and the tutor asked me if there was anything that I'd like to do but couldn't do. After a moment of thought I said that I liked the idea of doing a Skydive, but that I couldn't do it because I was afraid of heights. He replied in a gentle tone *"If you say you can't do it, you're right, you can't, but if you say you can, you can."*

It was the last day of the course and I listened to his reply, and didn't pay it much more attention until the car journey home. It was a two hour drive and what he had said to me kept going round in my brain: *"If you say you can't do it, you're right, you can't, but if you say you can, you can"*. It dawned on me on the drive home that, just perhaps, I could do it.

A couple of years later I was in Africa with friends and there was an opportunity for me to do a tandem skydive, and so with a deep breath and a shaky hand. I put my name down.

So there I was, the following morning, holding onto the wing of the plane hurtling along high in the sky. I had already stepped out of the plane door and edged my way along the right wing of the plane and was hanging there, my fingers gripping the front of the wing. Scared and wondering whether I was about to die. After a bit of persuasion from the instructor, I released my grip on the wing of the plane, let go, and fell down towards the beautiful Namibian sand dunes below. I was suddenly filled with the most amazing emotions of joy, happiness and fulfillment. It was a truly amazing experience that I will never forget and was honestly one of the best things I've ever done. I recommend it.

If you say you can, you can. It's true!

Sometimes you try something and it doesn't work out. Oh well, these things happen and at least you have learnt something. It's better to regret something you have done, than to regret something you haven't. It is not the critic who counts, or the person who points out how the strong stumbled, the credit belongs to the person who has actually tried to do something and failed. That person is infinitely better than the person who didn't bother. Try, try and try again. You only fail when you stop trying.

When it snows in the UK, problems occur. Nobody knows exactly where the snow will fall, how deep it will get or how icy the roads will become. Snow, in line with other weather phenomenon is chaotic and the wind blows the snow around and the flakes land where they fall. Problems happen, cars slide, trains are cancelled, people slip over and accidents increase.

It is a bit like life...we get what we're given and we can choose how we deal with whatever comes our way. Life isn't fair and for some people, snow is terrible and causes problems, for others it is beautiful and magical. You can choose to see it both ways.

There is wonder to imperfection. The Japanese have a phrase "*Wabi Sabi*" which relates to appreciating flaws, and to accept that there is beauty in unique differences. We are all different, nobody is perfect, and so to accept our own blemishes can be a marvellous thing. We are just fine as we are and there is no need to seek perfection. The flaws add value. We cannot change our past or who we are; we can only try to be our best selves in the future, and accept our defects...after all these things make us unique.

There are times in life when you feel like you have little choice and one of these periods is when you're at school. I used to work at a company that developed a School Management system, and I was responsible for the Attendance aspects, so I do appreciate how important school attendance is. There is a lot of focus on monitoring, reporting and improving attendance rates. The reason for this is because there is a clear and measurable correlation between good attendance and good results.

If a school has poor attendance it will result in poor results, it is as simple as that. If a child does not attend school for any reason then it disrupts their progress and also that of the other children in the class and it also impacts the teacher. When several children have time off it compounds this further and the results drop. Of course sometimes, if a child is ill, they should have the day off, however if a child can go in, then they should, it helps them and others.

From the age of 5 until 16 school is mandatory (in England anyway), and so during these 11 years, a child has to spend 190 days per year at school, which is just over two thousand days in total. This sounds a lot, and indeed it is, and it is a period of time that can transform you. I didn't particularly enjoy school myself but I tried to work hard and enjoyed some aspects of it, and I did okay in the end. For me, it was when I left school and went to college that I found learning more stimulating and then I wished I'd worked harder at school!

My opinion is that, because school is mandatory, you have to attend, and so you might as well give it your best shot. There is no point doing as little as possible, because you will literally be wasting your time, and you don't get to go home any earlier, and so you might as well work hard, try to learn as much as you can and enjoy it (as much as is possible). All being well you will then do better at your exams and actually come out with something worthwhile and for you to feel proud of yourself.

Believe me, when you are older and look back at your time at school, you will probably accept that it was one of the happiest times of your life, a time when you had few real responsibilities and pressures. Yes school can be hard work, demanding, and stressful, but please understand that this is giving you coping skills for the future, as you are continuously learning. Remember that all old people were young once.

Try to be kind and helpful.

Remember that every day is a **NEW** day.

Try to do something NEW <u>every day</u>.

- **N**ice. Do something kind and helpful for someone else. Make someone smile every day;

- **E**xercise – your body is amazing. Keep yourself fit and healthy by using it and stretching it daily;

- **W**orthwhile. Do something useful and valuable every single day.

Alongside this, have fun and enjoy your life.

You will find that over the next days and weeks, opportunities will arise for you to shine and show just what you can do. People always find new ways to move forward, and you will to. If there is something that you'd like to do, then what is stopping you?

Some people make things happen, some people watch things happen and some people wonder what happened. Try to be someone who makes things happen, and try to be that person from today. If you do what you've always done, you'll get what you've always got, and so try to do something different today. What's the harm, what's the worst that could happen? If you can accept the worst outcome, then anything better should be okay, and let's face it, if you are trying to do something positive the most likely outcome is a positive one.

A friend said to me that *"Ships are safest in the harbour, but that's not what they're built for"* and I think it's a powerful saying. For me it makes me think about how easy it is to just do the same things that you've always done, and how, if you try to do something different, although it can be scary, it can be quite amazing, and you can discover new lands!

Some people say do the thing that you fear, or do one thing each day that scares you. I think this makes sense to a point and I would suggest you take one new step forward each day and try something slightly outside of your comfort zone, and soon your comfort zone will grow bigger. Soon you will be able to do a lot more. You have your canvas, brush and colours, you paint paradise and in you go!

Remember, those who try to do something and fail are infinitely better than those who try nothing and succeed. Some people say that the way people behave compares with eagles and ducks. The concept is that eagles are strong, confident and powerful, they fly high and watch from above, protect their family, take their time and hunt selectively. They tend to be individuals and make their own decisions. Whereas ducks tend to be weaker, quite vulnerable, can hardly fly and make a lot of noise. Basically the idea is that you should try to be an eagle!

There are many ducks around, wasting time complaining and blaming others, try to fly high above them. Be an eagle.

Some say that we remember 20% of what we hear, 30% of what we see and hear, 70% of what we say and write, and 90% of what we do. The learning is in the doing. If you want to understand, try doing it. Remember that if one person can do something then you probably can do it too.

I came up with a simple acronym as follows: **ABC** …

- **A** for Action – Take action and do something;

- **B** for Belief – Have trust in your own ability and feel confident that you can do it;

- **C** for Check – Monitor your progress, and check that you are moving forward. Are you? If not. Go back to A and try an alternative approach.

It's as simple as **ABC**… Action, Belief, Check.

T

Key Points

➢ You are the latest version of all of your ancestors, improved over millions of years of evolution.

➢ If there is something you want to do, give it a try!

➢ Think *"Wabi Sabi"* and appreciate the flaws. They are what makes things unique and special.

➢ Work hard.

➢ Every day...

   ➢ **N** - Nice   (Do something nice for someone else)
   ➢ **E** - Exercise (Just 15 minutes will do!)
   ➢ **W** - Worthwhile   (Do something really useful)

➢ When you want to do something...

   ➢ **A** - Action   (Take action)
   ➢ **B** - Belief   (Believe in yourself and be confident)
   ➢ **C** - Check   (confirm progress is being made)

COMMUNICATIONS

As human beings we are communicating all the time, even when we're not doing anything, it's still giving a message to others. The way we communicate is vital and it is important what words we use when we speak, but did you know that the actual words we speak only represent about **7%** of the communication?

It sounds a bit ridiculous, but according to research done back in 1967 (the year I was born strangely enough) only around 7% of the message relates to the actual verbal content.

So what about the remaining 93%?

The next biggest chunk relates to the **tone** of the voice, which is around **38%**. This means that the tone of your voice, the *way* you say the words, is five times more powerful than *what* you say.

This can be demonstrated by saying something like *"I'm really happy"* in a sad tone. The words are almost meaningless.

This leaves **55%** of the communication to, Body Language! Yes the way you look, your stance, your facial expressions, eye contact, hand and arm movements, the way you sit or stand or move. Your body is unconsciously sending a very detailed communication of your feelings and emotions, which are being picked up by other people unconsciously.

This can be demonstrated by saying something like "*I'm really confident*" in a strong tone of voice with slumped shoulders and no eye contact – your body language overrides your words and tone of voice.

So, my message to you is that you should try to use your whole body to convey your message and be true to yourself, because whatever you really think will come through in your body language, and so be straight and congruent with your message.

First impressions are really important, and so if you want to convey a confident message, stand tall, with good eye contact and smile. Most of what you are communicating is here in your body language, before you even say a single word.

Know that your body is an effective indicator of your mood, and so try to behave as you would want people to see you. The nice thing is that, when your body is behaving in a certain way (e.g. with confidence), then you will also start to feel the same way inside, and your tone of voice will change accordingly.

NEXT STEPS

1. Get to the POINT

Think about what the **POINT** means in your world. What connections can you make with it, and what positive steps can you take to move forward?

- Purpose (what is yours?)
- Outcomes (what are yours?)
- Interests (what are yours?)
- Notice (what is happening?)
- Try (give it a go!)

Take out a blank piece of paper. Write "**The POINT**" at the top and then underneath that write **Purpose**. You now have your pen and paper and can begin to define the rest of your life…

2. Remind yourself of it every morning

Try to get into the routine of thinking about the **POINT** every day, as it will then become a habit. Just one aspect perhaps, anything that you think might help you to add focus to your day, everyday.

Consider the **NEW** approach of doing something **N**ice, **E**nergetic and **W**orthwhile every day.

Consider **ABC** – **A**ction, **B**elief and **C**heck.

3. Live your life your way

Try hard to follow your own path. The direction that you honestly think is a positive way forward for you. Have respect for others and what they think is important for you, but mostly respect your own opinion.

The person that you should listen to the most is yourself, because you know yourself better than anyone else, and this is the only way to true happiness. Alongside this, accept and appreciate imperfection.

THE END?

It is the end, for now anyway, or is it just the beginning?

At the start of this book I said that *"every journey starts with the first step"*, and you have done that, so thank you for coming along for the ride. I was initially referring to opening the book, and so now hopefully you have also chosen to read the entire book, and here we are at the end.

This is not the end, this is the beginning, a fresh start for you to embrace your dreams and desires, I wish you all the very best as you take your next steps.

I hope that this book has given you some food for thought and I sincerely hope that you will consider trying to use **POINT** to focus on your Purpose, Outcomes, Interests, to Notice more and to Try. You have the capability of transforming your life, only you can do it, it is your choice.

If you say you can, you can.

It is there, waiting.

TEN *"WISE"* SAYINGS

1. Do not walk behind me, for I may not lead. Do not walk ahead of me, for I may not follow. Do not walk beside me either, just leave me alone!

2. Always remember that you are unique, just like everyone else.

3. Never test the depth of water with both feet.

4. It may be that your sole purpose in life is simply to serve as a warning to others.

5. Before you criticise someone, walk a mile in their shoes. That way, when you criticise them, you're a mile away and you have their shoes.

6. If at first you don't succeed, skydiving isn't for you.

7. Give a man a fish and he will eat for a day. Teach him how to fish and he will sit in a boat all day and drink beer.

8. If you lend someone £20 and never see them again, it was worth it.

9. The quickest way to double your money is to fold it in half and put it back in your pocket.

10. If you keep your head when all around you are losing theirs and blaming it on you, then you are an axe murderer.

WHAT IS THE POINT? SONG

Chorus

What is the point? Where are we going?

It starts to appear when the purpose is clear

What is the point? What's it all about?

Focus on the outcome and you will soon find out.

Verse 1

You need targets to focus your mind

Set some goals to achieve, objectives defined

Keep interested in what's going on

You'll begin to see as time moves on

Chorus

Verse 2

What do you notice about yourself?

All around you information is wealth

Try to take another step each day

You'll get further forward. It's the only way

Chorus

Verse 3

Today is a brand new start

Take a step forward and follow your heart

There's so much to see and do

Wabi Sabi my friend, it's up to you!

Chorus

What is the point? Where are we going?

It starts to appear when the purpose is clear

What is the point? What's it all about?

Dreams are in the making you're about to find out.

…see if you can find this song on YouTube

ABOUT THE AUTHOR

Jon lane is a son, husband and father, living in Bedford, trying to make the most of life.

An IT manager, NLP Practitioner and guitar player, who also enjoys running, swimming and playing squash (but not at the same time).

I am very lucky to have some wonderful family and friends in my life, and to have the freedom and good health to be able to do so many things that I enjoy. I think that life is a fascinating adventure.

Printed in Great Britain
by Amazon

ALIVE IN PARTS OF THIS CENTURY: ERIC MOTTRAM AT 70

alive in parts of this century:

Eric Mottram
at 70

ALIVE IN PARTS OF THIS CENTURY:

ERIC MOTTRAM AT 70

Edited by Peterjon and Yasmin Skelt

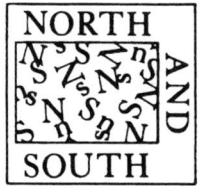

Twickenham and Wakefield

Published in November 1994 by North and South at
23 Egerton Road, Twickenham, Middlesex TW2 7SL and at
3 Westfield Park, College Grove, Wakefield, West Yorkshire WF1 3RP

The publishers gratefully acknowledge: Dale Carter for provision of the
tape from which Howell Daniels' text was transcribed and Nia and Lowri
Daniels for permission to publish it; Eric Mottram for the photographs at
Vicarage Gate, University of Warwick, the Miners' Benefit, Regent's
College, the Sorbonne and the rocking stone; Enitharmon Press, which
published Sandra Fisher's drawing in *Monotypes & Tracings* in 1994; Peter
Finch for a large number of sticky red dots.

Title: "alive in parts of this century" is the opening line of 'Interrogation
Rooms 15' by Eric Mottram.

Cover: Eric Mottram on a rocking stone in Derbyshire, England, late 1980s.
Photograph by David Murray.

Frontispiece: **PETER DONNELLY**

Printed by the K & N Press Ltd, 142 Molesey Avenue, West Molesey,
Surrey KT8 2RY.

ISBN 1 870314 26 3

British Library Cataloguing-in-Publication Data.
A catalogue record for this book is available from the British Library.

FOREWORD

Professor Eric Mottram is 70 on 29th December 1994 and this book was made to honour and congratulate him; Eric at 70: "hard to accept" as Iain Sinclair writes here.

The book brings together works from friends who are writers, artists, ex-students, colleagues or all of these, to celebrate a true phenomenon. The vast range of material here highlights many facets of Eric. There is the teacher who could seem "difficult and fiery", or arrive with a "booming guffaw", or take the care to find a chair for a late arrival at his lecture. There is the poet whose words are "calm and learned", but whose "rhythms are angry, the anger that goes into Blake's 'mental fight'". There is the passionate defender against oppression of writers and booksellers, into the law courts as necessary. There is the musician, cook, traveller, editor; and time and again there is the loyal and generous friend.

These facets will be recognised by all who know Eric Mottram. For those who do not, the strength, richness and enthusiasm here provide an introduction and an invitation to explore further. Professor Mottram's publications to date include some fifty books, evenly divided between critical works and poetry, and nearly two hundred essays in periodicals and anthologies worldwide.

It has been a pleasure and an adventure to make this book and we thank all the contributors, benefactors and subscribers who have made it possible. Among those who have provided valuable assistance at various stages of the project, we wish to thank John Whiting particularly for his unfailing un-common sense, thoughtful advice and great good humour.

Yasmin Skelt
Peterjon Skelt
David Annwn

North and South

Eric Mottram has given hedonism a good name. Having discovered that the purpose of life is pleasure, and that the greatest pleasure derives from sharing with the world the enthusiastic cultivation of all one's faculties, he set out to teach to as many as possible the finer points of judicious, enlightened, generous and joyful sensuality. Among the tools of his trade are anger and laughter: anger at the stupidity of greed, envy and invincible ignorance (as packaged and peddled by our bosses through their media), and laughter welling up from the astounding reciprocal delights of discovery and recognition. The lesson he teaches through his poetry, his lectures and his life is that *joie de vivre* is indivisible and that the pleasures of the ear and the eye, the seminar and the kitchen, the page and the stage – all are wholly symbiotic.

Universities, like vintners, must give distinctive labels to their fermentations, so this is called "cultural studies". But the phrase doesn't begin to convey the exhilaration of a day spent conversing, hearing, watching, eating and drinking in Eric's company. If it is true – and it *must* be true – that every improvement one makes in the quality of another's life enriches one's own, then Eric should be one of the happiest of mortals. May his joy, and that of his readers, his students and his friends, continue to proliferate.

LAWRENCE FERLINGHETTI, A Flight Through Time

For Eric Mottram at 70

Wearing Apollinaire's derby I am in a zeppelin with a
hundred dignitaries in tailcoats from all over the
world cruising about looking for a place to declare
peace looking for a soft landing for peace on earth
Gardens are sighted on the horizon and the airship
veers in that direction only to discover there is no
airfield and we veer off again The sky is lit with flares
A man in tails with wings jumps off the Eiffel tower
thinking he's a bird He plummets straight down in front
of his friends I am picking petals off a sunflower in
Provence It's midsummer A million crickets sound their
huge drone in the night A sunflower leans in a window
where I am a boy leaning out Loulou Loulou someone calls
I have picked all the petals They fall Loulou Loulou
Où es-tu It is hot in the dark room There are riots in
France and Italy The Americans killed Sacco and Vanzetti
I saw Lindberg land The zeppelin sails on There is jazz
on the radio It's Sidney Bechet Paris 1930s the dignitaries
toasting each other in champagne and American cigarettes
The pilot sends a Morse code greeting to a ship at sea
The band plays on The Captain sends back a round of drinks
on the house sailing through the hot night an endless flight
around the world We gaze out the portals of the gondola
at the endless stars Night reveals the cities of earth
lit with leftover sun I am kneeling in short pants in a
cathedral somewhere in France Christ died on Friday and
rose on Sunday setting a world altitude record out of
sight in the dark firmament I don't believe a word of it
The wine doesn't taste like blood The dirigible soars in
the summit of heaven Where will it ever land The eternal
pilot pores over the charts The dawn is pointing On a lake
far below the wood boats knock together Life sails on I am
stretched out in a sailing-canoe in upstate New York An
eagle soars in the summit of heaven An opera hat lies on
a marble table in the lobby of the Paris opera High over
the city a plane searches the sky making a sound like a
gnat It's a plane it's a bird it's a man There is a thrill
in the air We are walking down the Avenue de l'Opèra The
Metro entrance yawns with its art-deco mouth and swallows us

The zeppelin flies on into the twenty-first century The
zeppelin is life itself The zone we fly through endless
without borders without boundaries There are no more nations
Ethnic hordes sweep the earth in search of food and shelter
We throw down our champagne glasses The tv shows the endless
night sky We are watching an eclipse The universe endless
stretches away in the night There must be a place where
all is light Where then O Endless One in endless eternity
Where now We are heavenly bodies rapt in time hurtling through
bent space Flame-outs illuminate the landscape

I cannot remember precisely when I first met Eric Mottram in 1947. We were fellow students at Cambridge in the same college, Pembroke. May be it was his intense bursting forth of laughter that first attracted my attention, or his staccato machine gun like delivery of words, followed by pauses to check whether the verbal message had struck home, or not. If not, then another burst, to ensure the verbal target had been hit with accuracy. One's answer had to be sound.

I, at once, recognised a shared dislike of posturing in the name of importance in Eric and a disciplined mind that could separate falsity and pomposity from true purpose a mile away. Eric attacked people posturing in bogus positions with words combined with laughter. In our hearts, we were both serious people, who cared about what we believed to be important. We remain so. We were young rebels who believed in our causes. The world however was to be taken apart kindly. We shared a belief that humour provides a very powerful dissecting knife, with which to tease out truth from the confusion of muddle mindedness, and to achieve social progress. It hurts less to do things this way. Our causes were more important to us than the social need to be labelled rebels. As heretics we were too wise, and enjoyed life too much, to wish to be burned at the stake. We had seen too many heroes perish.

Like others, we were two young post war veterans, moving on from constrained but, for our age, considerable military responsibility. The war had taught us survival was a virtue. We had the huge pleasure of exchanging the life of military discipline for the liberty and joy of educating ourselves in the marvellous architectural environment of Cambridge.

After years of military discipline, the capacity to travel where one wished in the vacations to see what one wanted, was indeed a liberty. Military service involved much forced international travel, for example, in Eric's case on the freezing seas on the route to Archangel. Our friendship was eventually to exploit this liberty to the full. Travel was simply a matter of money and choice. I suppose we saw the challenge as a simple one. It was to turn ourselves into Renaissance men in a vacation or two on less than £70 all in. Quite a challenge for a retired lieutenant from the Navy, studying English, and a retired Captain from the Army studying Natural Sciences. Among our influences was Professor Pevsner then Slade Professor of Fine Art at Cambridge, who helped us form our ideas about architecture.

Our travels were to be based on architecture and the visual arts. Dante could be read at home, as well as Vergil. The visual thread that links Eric, as an American English scholar, forward into photography, and myself, as a Natural Scientist, forward into the teaching of architecture and environment for thirty years, was first nurtured in those travels.

In my last year at Cambridge we planned our Grand Tour to Italy with some care. At my suggestion, we decided we would systematically visit all the Pierro della Francesca paintings in Italy. We would add in the great northern cities of Mantua, Padua, Verona and Vicenza. It was essential to visit Palladian architecture. En route we could add in Rimini and Ravenna, and acquire some feeling for Byzantine architecture. Assisi was also en route, a more Gothic experience.

All student travel in those days was by train. There was the crossing of the channel by the longest slowest and cheapest boat route. The long train journey through Europe, crisp ham rolls through the window at various stops, until suddenly, in Switzerland, one became alive to the adventure of travel from the marvellous mountain views, and so on into Italy. Milan station was always a complicated spot for students, because they tended to take the train apart there and reassemble it in various undeclared ways, shunting bits and pieces here and there. If one went for a snack, it was a major problem to relocate one's seat and luggage in a specific train. Successful in finding our bags, we pushed on through Florence to Arezzo. The cheapest stopping point was in the hotel above the bus station, where we were sleeplessly deafened all night long.

We started on our cultural mission viewing the Francesca fresco cycle of the story of the true cross in the Church of San Francesco. We were magnificently impressed.

After Arezzo, we set off for Borgo San Sepolcro to view the Resurrection in the Palazzo Comunale. On the wall of the municipal office, in days of more modest tourism, one talked one's way in among the humble bureaucrats and their papers. Our guide, a clerk, taking time off his duties, told us of a visit by Sir Kenneth Clarke, who had tried to persuade them they were too poor to look after it properly, and that logically its true home was the National Gallery in London, where it would be properly cared for. Italian good sense fortunately prevailed in the face of the relative poverty of Italy after the war.

We had a long wait through the heat of the day for our onward bus. We camped out in the shade under the trees with a large hunk of Parmesan cheese, and a piece of bread, and waited for the heat to yield. There were many such hot afternoons of waiting.

On arrival at each destination, one first of all had to find somewhere cheap to stay. Then there was the need for food. Eating out on travel with Eric was always difficult. His taste for good food and wine was always tempered by his strong dislike of having to pay enough actually to get it. There was always the most massive evening search for the cheapest good restaurant in town. The debate about potential versus price was endless. Eventually, exhausted, we sat down, having doubled our appetite and thirst in the searching, and hoped tomorrow would be better. Sometimes we would just buy fruit and grapes, and not search at all, but eat instead in the street. That was restful.

So we proceeded on by bus, missed train connections, and on foot to the remote cemetery in Monterchi, more ambitiously to Assisi, and eventually across the hills to Urbino. There, at last, we really felt we had arrived in the Renaissance, and were now indeed "true Renaissance men". Our purse strings were relaxed for two days. We stayed in a hotel two stars up market of our normal. This was civilisation. We were civilised. We ate relatively expensively to keep up with the Lorenzos and Federigo da Montefeltros of the historic world. We felt we must spend enough money to enjoy it properly.

However such good times could not last, and soon we had slipped back two stars in hotels, and the long evening hunt for the cheapest best food in town resumed. In Rimini and Ravenna we were able to visit the early Byzantine churches. Then it was Padua, with the magnificent frescoes of Giotto. I recall well our evening stroll in Vicenza to view the Palladian Villa Rotunda.

Reflecting, I also remember our visit to the Palladian theatre, structured by perspective. Little could I imagine then that in the course of time I was to father a competent playwright, Louise Page. In those days, there were few women in Cambridge University. We thought about Renaissance men. Renaissance women lay outside our ken. We were not prejudiced but merely untutored, and inexperienced. We had lived in Armies and Navies without women about for over four years before Cambridge, and in Cambridge too. I have a vivid memory in the train going to Mantua, of laughing ourselves silly about an Italian written English Guide blurb. This included a statement about poor Julio de Romano "flushing his lavish genius all over the ceiling". The Italian ticket collector was surprised to find two Englishmen travelling with so much rollicking laughter. He obviously thought until then we were a subdued race.

Perhaps the biggest personal renaissance revelation of the trip for me was the work of Mantegna in Mantua.

So loaded with memories, visually more experienced, our money exhausted, we returned home on the long train journey, less money now for ham rolls at station stops. On the way, the mountains of Switzerland were still luring us, now moneyless, through the window, to jump off. But that would have led us into romanticism. So refreshed, the two new Renaissance men returned to University.

The issue, since, for us both, has been how to avoid establishing ourselves in defined narrow disciplines. We have tried instead to discipline our whole range of ideas within the widest structures of human life. Our aim has been to enrich life in a total sense. We have remained Renaissance men, in a world that over partitions people into narrow specialisms of scholarship.

As Pierro della Francesca knew, choosing one's point of perspective is really important.

GAVIN SELERIE, In Melville's Track

A Jack is in the stars, spangled
in reels out of a toy-box: may must
ride it through, cinders blowing back
on the collar, a three-mile grade
to sing with a spiker's echo
jump-a, rattle and roll, from a cold iron bunk
or a labyrinth of filing cabinets.

Hunter at sea, a cluster striding
in stark December, shines
a red shoulder — a blue-white foot.

A civil heart won't drive meanness away:
the civic calls for a lightning mix,
a fit at full-finger speed. Word-warm
readies the cut of the point above.

There's a hidden side to Eric Mottram – hidden even to himself – and that is his letters. They were almost always painstakingly written in his minuscule hand, covering often several pages at a time; they answered every minor point and teemed with seething comments on people, places and the cultural scene. They also contain the only insights into his own personality and life, a life he has practically kept private, never wishing to impose his own suffering as ballast in a budding friendship. At various moments, they were also my only connection to the world. The first dates from September 1957, but from 1973 to 1989, they were few and far between. Here are some out-of-context excerpts.

September 3, 1957: "Dear Wignesan, ... I hope you can understand that my criticalness is part of my deep feeling and concern for the things of literature which seem to me to matter, not just wind and inability to appreciate anything. [E.M. taught at the University of Malaya in Singapore from 1953 to '55] ... You make me mad saying that modern poetry and literature is [sic] neglected. My first year tutorial students know of "Prufrock", and my honours degree group studied Eliot, Yeats, Orwell, Hemingway, Faulkner, Penn Warren, Wallace Stevens, Joyce and Pound. The examination paper gave them a chance to show their knowledge of a number of other writers if they wanted to – the choice and encouragement was enormous. You may say that this was only for about a dozen men and girls: but I'd remind you that 20th. century literature is difficult for a fairly decently educated European, and that these advanced students worked hard with extraordinary enthusiasm. You are also wrong about the other literature taught. I myself lectured on the nineteenth and twentieth centuries, from the Romantics to the 1950s; but there were other courses covering literature from Chaucer right through to the 18th. century. [...] But let's be realistic about writers: they write in their own cultures in an intensely closed-in way; they are solitary, selfish, incapable of turning on the tap of being interested in what they are not, hating to simulate what does not concern their inner peculiar experience. [...] After all, English writers are not gregarious like the French, for instance. [Here E.M. comments juicily on Lin Yu-tang] The only recent example of an English writer in the East is Graham Greene in Indo-China, resulting in some good articles in the newspapers and one of his best novels, "The Quiet American". He went as a paid newspaper reporter for a limited period. [...] I'm enjoying this letter because I can talk at you without being interrupted.

This is a very bleak place... All around stretches an endless flat land and to the south the great expanses of sea and sky and cloud. The sun does not shine and it rains in the night, but I find it soothing and relaxing. My nerves have shaken themselves free. It takes a true egoist to enjoy such solitude." (replying to a paper I gave at the *Malayan Independence Conference* in London, August 1957, from Caravan X6, Sea-Front Caravan park, Mill Farm, Selsey, Sussex)

February 4, 1958: "The thought of having to put up with your arguments for more than one hour fills me with panic, I may add; I'm beginning to see how intolerant and emotional I am, and I don't like it. So let me do penance by reading your revised poems! [...] I wonder if you have managed in Berlin to come across a prize-winning Indian film called "Pather Panchali": it is undoubtedly a masterpiece by any standards. The director is a young man named Satyajit Ray: it's his first film, astonishingly enough. [...] I lead a very tied existence for no good reason I sometimes think. My poems lie in a folder unfinished, like all my other creative writing: a pity this. I think the time has come for another move, a change, in my life: I've been still for three years. Here's a poem – unrevized – on lecturing: it's as good a subject as any: and it's called the 'Lecture in the Cave.'" (from A-weg 39, Gröningen, The Netherlands)

March 11, 1958: "... I'm apologetic about the myth references in that awful poem which I sent you in a brief moment of uninhibitedness: but it is a European poem and I have a right to my European myths. I agree that it's a pretty cheap way with metaphor: but then I'm no great shakes as a poet of course. [...] If we use myth to eke out our own metaphors and images, this is what happens: incommunicability between cultures. The difference is that I want my thing read by Europeans not Asians: you want both. [...] I must say the influence of Anderson [the Canadian poet who taught literature in Singapore in the early fifties] on the imitative Malayans grows worse and worse the more I hear about it. After all, what has he produced of value? An obscure book of poems (not published in England) and two pieces of scandal-ridden autobiography, which I liked; but this is minor stuff. The only help a European can give to a Malayan is, first, a truthful knowledge of European experience today and in the past, and second, to try to sharpen his awareness of what his problems are, how Malayan life can get its literature, what kind of language to use. Nothing else is useful. The meteoric appearance of minor poets and their curiously individual daily life, is no more than a freak show. [...] The inability of Malayans to understand themselves adds to the social chaos which is easily the obvious hallmark of the place. [...] About Dylan Thomas, don't forget he married, had children, settled in a house, tried to accept the double responsibility of being a man and a poet, tried to make money by art, and drank himself to death. [...] His prose and poetry styles are strictly inimitable: don't even be slightly influenced or it will show immediately. But have your London life of lurking and walking by all means – it's traditional. It's beyond my capacity to be so unselfconscious." (from Gröningen)

June 29, 1958: "...I did not expect so much frankness all at once. I am myself incapable of it, and although I bitterly expect it from my friends, I have no right to what I can't do myself. My only justification is this: no one has ever expected me to explain myself. It sometimes seems to me that I have been doing little else these last fifteen years but listen and then speak out as decently as I could or wanted to. I want to know and feel people, but I have found little such curiosity, at least to such an intensity, in others; so you can see how you came to be the victim of my – I now see - rather abrupt interrogations." (from Gröningen)

August 8, 1958: "... I am struggling to read "The Outsider" which I gave up in boredom and irritation last year and have begun again in deference to yourself. Camus's "The Rebel" seems to me a much more original contribution to our times. But I enormously enjoyed your account of meeting Wilson – only let me say, you really must be more critical of these personalities. Obviously Wilson appeals to your own rebelliousness – but for goodness' sake don't become a rebel's minion! There's something deeply conservative in poetry: rebellion in the arts is always a disguise for a profound human continuity, isn't it?"

February 2, 1959: "... My mother has sold the old house and moved to Brighton, ... [...] I don't much like being far from London when I am in England, but that's the way it will be now. [...] The proofs of a poem to be put out in the US came and went: it made me a bit courageous for a while, especially as I am to be paid – actually paid – however trivial the sum is - it makes you feel professional, which is entirely flattering to the self because I am not, and know it. I have been reading a poet I admire very much and would like you to read – a young American called Lawrence Ferlinghetti – you can read him in "Pictures of the Gone World" or "A Coney Island of the Mind". I even have a record of him and other US boys reading their stuff. I'm going to talk about him to my students the week after next. By the way, I heard Dom Moraes reading his stuff on the Third last night: [two juicy lines just have to be dropped] ...He has talent but at the moment it sounds like some one else's he has appropriated. Like John Press.
You'll laugh to know that I am taking part in a seminar on Ayer's book [The Problem of Knowledge] we looked at together – fortnight after fortnight all last term and now this – unravelling that mind! It'll be engraved on my soul like Calais or callous. Pity you weren't there to be done good to!" (from Gröningen)

May 20, 1959: "...I always understand your silences, if you mean I realize you are like me in writing letters nearly always on the spur of the moment, a sort of emotional crisis in a minor way." (from Gröningen)

October 12, 1959: "... Might not your struggle for sheer independence be an illusion: no man who marries for children wants independence surely: not unless he simply means irresponsibility. For instance, I don't marry because I don't think I could love a girl enough to make her happy enough to justify making her so dependent. I'm probably merely the prey to neurosis, but that's it just now. [...] ...we all need help, all being desperate potentially lonely men yelping to the empty air for love, which means dependence, which means work, which means the only comforts there are, God being either a cynical monster or simply a word without meaning.

Don't you really do more than survive? I have a feeling you do not fill your life with enough, and that part of your disease is emptiness: you have not the European desire for a complex and utterly *present* culture. Yearning for spiritual emptiness, nirvana, one-ness under the Bo-tree (I know you are not a Buddhist), refusal of the penetration of the arts, all of them, and nature. Are all Indians and Malayans Puritans? Probably yes. [...] About me, I have been appointed lecturer in English literature with special interest in American literature at London University, and I begin in January because my work here is such that it carries responsibilities. I just can't simply leave. It's a wonderful new job, and I'm lucky and grateful about it - especially in this competitive academic world we ratrace in. But I'm not that good and I'm wondering how long I'll last." (from Gröningen)

January 21, 1960: "... I can only look forward to having a literary talk again – the literary set don't seem to have been much use to you in London. But I think perhaps you expect writers to be writers all the time. But I also agree that the literary set wields atrocious power in England. Poetry has to be in the modes agreed upon to get far towards publishing. I myself find it extremely difficult to recognize the new and valuable, so entrenched in patterns of the recognizable does one become. Open mind seems to be not enough – even an ironic pose which really stems from patronizing superiority!

In a way I'm jealous of your being on terms with Colin Wilson, Spender, Enright, and so on, although I do not admire anything they've done except early Spender poems and Enright's essays on Rilke and Goethe. Surely you are on the right track to be healthily sceptical of these eminences in a flat land. [...] The only poetry I've read recently that might interest you is Robert Lowell's "Life Studies" which is a fine achievement I think. His use of flexible rhythms in long lines will interest you.

Why John Press? Not surely because I reviewed his earliest critical book very critically! I don't suppose I told you any way. He's a pretty awful poet – has all the clichés of other poets, a sort of idle Georgian whose [sic] read Eliot and Auden, but who can't help letting his rubbishy romantic naturism poke washily through. Who is John Press, by the way?" (from King's College, London)

March 19, 1960: "... I think your view of poetry in England a shade pessimistic; Ted Hughes has just had a new volume out, and every week or so some new volume by new or relatively unknown poets seems to appear – and the host of poetry-publishing little journals is quite large – a glance in Zwemmer's would confirm this. [...] "Listen" ["Listener"?]... is associated with the group of Philip Larkin, Kingsley Amis, Donald Davie. They like precision, clear forms, intellectual content... (They refused my only poems I sent them!)" (from King's College, London)

October 22, 1960: "... I have never believed that suffering is good for a man necessarily and never will. [...] I have one or two addresses of publishers of tiny output – I mean they do it for love. One of the striking things in America is this getting on with publishing at your own expense. I met a couple, poor and clever, who "work" a little and then bring out irregularly a magazine called "Birth" which they hawk at street corners until it's time to "work" again – to get money to live and bring out "Birth" - he's an oriental-looking Jewish fellow with masses of dark curly beard, she's a lovely lithe creature with [a] lovely sense of humour and lack of affectation.

I brought back stacks of American poetry; I met Ferlinghetti, Ginsberg, Herbert Gold, Seymour Krim, and others: and toured thousands of miles meeting hundreds of people, and discovering I hope truth. And now I want to get it into my lectures, into writing, I might even make poems again and stop being sterile and dull. New blood around; it's done me good; justice must now be done. [...] Up to here in work now the university year has begun, with lectures and so on, review-writing, courses in other colleges, Times Literary Supplement stuff, etc. etc. I've never been so busy. So should you come over, leave a message at King's, will you. Meanwhile, as ever – Eric" (from King's College, London, on returning from his first trip to the States)

TED WILENTZ, For Eric Mottram on his 70th Birthday

If you push the Eric Mottram button in my mind, a picture unfolds of Eric bounding upstairs where I await him at the door of my Greenwich Village apartment. He would be beaming, an expression of the energy and zest so characteristic of him and, I like to think, from sharing my anticipation of meeting again a newly-found friend. It is a picture that has stayed with me since 1960 when he made his first trip to the United States during which we first met.

Perhaps because I was reading Kafka's *Amerika* about that time, I always relate Eric to him though they make an odd pair. Kafka wrote *Amerika* never having been here, creating a symbolic country that existed only in his imagination. Eric, too, seemed fascinated by the United States even before he ever visited it but he lectured and wrote about American literature and society with an astonishing knowledge and sense of reality. This so impressed our State Department that it sponsored his trip to contribute to Anglo-American cultural relationships by enabling him to better understand America and to exchange ideas and opinions with scholars, writers and Americans generally.

Allowed to arrange his own two and a half months itinerary, Eric went to historic sites and towns, to universities and to centers of the new in writing and the arts. In San Francisco, he visited City Lights Books and had a long talk with Lawrence Ferlinghetti who gave him my name as a possible help for Eric in New York City in meeting writers and extending his awareness of the movements and happenings that were part of a dramatic change in our culture and society. This being 1960, Ferlinghetti represented a radical break from the establishment and from the academic world. Years later, I realized how unorthodox Eric's travels among the avant-garde would have seemed to his academic colleagues when he told me, with a rare bitterness, that when they asked him his field and he said American literature, they were likely to ask, "Oh. Is there an American literature?".

Since 1960, Eric has published a good deal of poetry, criticism and essays. He has come to the United States every so often, invited by various universities as a visiting professor. It has been a great pleasure to my wife, Joan, and to me that he would come to see us when in this country, sometimes staying a few days.

I try to think of Eric's and my first meeting but the details have faded while the memory of an immediate rapport remains; one meeting creating a depth of friendship that made the length of it irrelevant. I do recall responding, as I still do, to Eric's warmth and enthusiasm, his widespread knowledge and interests and his strong concern for individuals and for humanity.

WILLIAM BURROUGHS, The Monkey Head

Everyman: "That's what everyman wants isn't it? TO BE GOD! Hell yes."
Genie: "You have the monkey's head and that allows you three wishes. So think carefully."
Everyman: "How can everyman go wrong? He's *God* for Christ sake. And how can God be wrong?"
Genie: "This is your wish? Then pick up the head and say aloud 'I want to have God powers'."
Everyman: "I want to have God powers. God damn it!!! He bit me!"
Genie: "No problem sire. Heal yourself."
Everyman: "Ah yes."
Genie: "And now sire a few problems require your attention. Even in a town of 60,000 people are born, they fall sick, they grow old, they die, they go insane, they kill themselves. For all this you must give detailed instructions and bear full responsibility. And remember you are not only all *knowing,* but all *feeling..* Shall we start in the terminal cancer ward where the Mets always win?"

An hour later.

Everyman: "My God I can't stand it.. I *feel* it, all of it. *I can't help feeling it..* Suppose I don't give any orders? What then?"
Genie: "Nothing will happen from here to Eternity."
Everyman: "All right. I want to give up my God powers. He bit me again.."
Genie: "There are a few people here who have some bones to pick with you.. Friends.. relatives.. look out there."

Faces of insane hate to the sky in all directions..

"THERE HE IS.. HE'S THE ONE.. LET'S GET HIM"

Everyman makes his last wish... "I want to be back where I was before the monkey stuck his head in."

Everyman is back in his dreary bed sitter.

When I say that studying American Literature with Eric changed my life, I mean this in more than the immediately obvious sense that, had I not been his student, I would not now be teaching and writing about American literature and living in the United States. Had it not been for Eric, it is most unlikely that I would have done *any* scholarly work in literature beyond the B.A., let alone have had an academic career. The following excerpts from 1963 letters home, from Bedford College, tell the story:

"I'm enjoying both my special subjects v. much indeed. The chap we have for American Lit. is v. keen & excitable & is a most stimulating person... v. few people do American Literature, so you get much more attention & more scope to be original."

"I went to a terrific lecture by Mr Mottram on Tuesday evening about William Burroughs. It turns out that he knows Burroughs personally. He came over to talk to me when he had finished & said that he was pleased I'd managed to come & then said to everyone that those who wanted to could go over the road to the 'Cheshire Cheese' where they would continue discussing Burroughs. Unfortunately I had to dash off & meet Adrienne & didn't think anymore about it until I walked into the seminar yesterday & the first thing he said to me was, 'Why didn't you come over to the Cheshire Cheese after the lecture, I was expecting you to?' I was very 'chuffed'. He is very encouraging if you let him see that you're interested in American Literature, especially someone like Burroughs, so I hope I'll have another opportunity to talk to him personally."

"I asked Mr Mottram if there was anything written about William Burroughs. He said there really wasn't but that soon he was having a book on him published in America & that as soon as possible he would get me a draft of it to read. I was 'wild with joy' – he's the leading authority on Am. Lit. in Britain & there we were talking about Burroughs like old friends & laughing uproariously – am I glad I did Am. Lit. – I would v. much like to do research in it, under him. It would be v. worth while."

I was not invited to do graduate work, yet Eric had made further study seem a real option. By treating me as someone who could hold up her side of a serious discussion of literature then, he encouraged me to assume that I could continue to do so in the future.

Within a few years, opportunities for women in academia would begin to open up a little, but in 1965, the "double standard" remained almost completely unquestioned, even in an all-women's college with several fine women professors. For women students, the code of extreme decorousness and deferentiality toward professors had the silent corollary of acquiescence in a whole set of unarticulated, severely limiting expectations.

This phenomenon is by now very well-known – in theory. Yet, for the women who graduated at any time before 1965 – for how long after, I was not around to know – it was an experience that they lived and that, for the vast majority of them, closed off any further scholarly possibilities. A woman student was encouraged to push herself to the top of her bent *until* she received her Bachelor's degree and then, with very few exceptions, was expected to "make herself scarce". If she wanted to marry and have children, she should consider this her "career". (Few of us, at London, could expect to be able to pay other people to raise our children.) I still remember vividly being told by a friend in the year ahead of mine how the woman professor who invited her to do graduate study cautioned her not to accept unless she was completely reconciled to forgoing marriage and a family.

Lest you wonder where Eric fits into all this – "decorousness" is one of the clues. He *was* such a powerful influence at that particular time because, in his attitudes, interests – and his demeanour – he was always somewhat "outside the system". It wasn't that he spoke out against the double standard, he just seemed to operate outside it – and in a way that for me, introduced an alternative set of expectations. Eric's extreme "infectious enthusiasm" for American literature had a particularly powerful "reorienting" effect. Its implicit message was: "There's a vast body of significant and challenging material here waiting to be discovered and a great deal of worthwhile work to be done with this material. Find out what's happening now. Keep an open mind. Be prepared to shift your perspectives in the light of new information and new experiences." What I internalized most from Eric's whole approach to scholarship was, "Show your enthusiasm, stick your neck out, go against the grain, get there a bit before the others. They won't understand what you are doing and they may try to be dismissive, or condescending, but eventually they will have to catch up with you."

By 1965 – the summer of Ginsberg's "International Poetry Incarnation" at the Albert Hall – Eric had given me what I needed to "go it alone". My first exposure to Ezra Pound, for example, came in the form of one of Eric's handouts, a two-sided typed sheet of excerpts from Canto 74 – which I still have. According to some Poundian principle of "natural increase", this poetic "seed" would germinate into two books of Pound criticism. He also taught me all I needed to know about canon-busting. Working in American literature in a British university in the mid-sixties – for the small number of students fortunate enough to be able to do this – was the best possible apprenticeship in giving underrated literatures their due. Within the changing cultural contexts in which I found myself teaching, over the years, the assumption that a great deal of valuable literature was waiting to be explored, continued to prove itself – in the early '70s with women's writing, then with African American, Native American, Gay and Lesbian, Latino/a, Asian American (and, this year, Arabic American) literature and culture.

Congratulations Eric, on your 70th birthday and your whole career. And very many thanks!

Facing page: **TOM RAWORTH,** For Eric

WILL ROWE, La mañana alza el río…

Translated from Emilio Adolfo Westphalen, Las ínsulas extrañas, *first published in Lima in 1933 and collected in* Otra imagen deleznable, *Mexico, 1980.*

Dear Eric,

You first asked me to translate some Latin American poetry for POETRY REVIEW, years ago, and I am grateful for that and subsequent encouragement and our many discussions of what it means to translate.

When things get difficult I enjoy it most. Westphalen is difficult in several ways. Spanish tends to be quite loud, to the immediate ear, and Westphalen's book explores what can start to happen when a certain degree of quietness is achieved. He produces an extreme softness which allows words and things to enter the body ecstatically. This is what's most difficult to translate. The other main feature is that he slows the language down, with an invitation to let go of those syntactic structures (more powerful in Spanish) that predict by laying out the ground ahead of one's attention.

I hope my version manages to convey some of this.

The morning offers river and hair
Then mist night
Sky eyes
Gaze at me eyes sky
To wake up without vertebrae without structure
The skin in its eternity
Softens becoming lost in memory
Existed did not exist
Along the path of eyes the path of sky
How tender the summer weeps in your mouth
Raining pleasure and joy
The sea brings in its love
Fears the rose the foot the skin
The sea takes away its love
The sea
How many boats
The waves speak of love
Again the mist another boat
The oars love does not move
Knows how to close the eyes sleep the air not the eyes
Wave reaching the eyes
Sleep beside river hair
Without danger of shipwreck in the eyes

Calm slowness the sky
Or eyes
Fire fire fire fire
In the sky sky fire sky
How the silence rolls
Over sky fire love silence
What torment drenches forehead silence
Behind absence you watched without fire
Is absence night
But eyes fire
Tenderness summer eyes mouth
Fire is born in the eyes
Love is born in eyes sky fire
Fire love silence

[La mañana alza el río la cabellera / Después la niebla la noche / El cielo los ojos / Me miran los ojos el cielo / Despertar sin vértebras sin estructura / La piel está en su eternidad / Se suaviza hasta perderse en la memoria / Existía no existía / Por el camino de los ojos por el camino del cielo / Qué tierno el estío llora en tu boca / Llueve gozo beatitud / El mar acerca su amor / Teme la rosa el pie la piel / El mar aleja su amor / El mar / Cuántas barcas / Las olas dicen amor / La niebla otra vez otra barca / Los remos el amor no se mueve / Sabe cerrar los ojos dormir el aire no los ojos / La ola alcanza los ojos / Duermen junto al río la cabellera / Sin peligro de naufragio en los ojos / Calma tardanza el cielo / O los ojos / Fuego fuego fuego fuego / En el cielo cielo fuego cielo / Cómo rueda el silencio / Por sobre el cielo el fuego el amor el silencia / Qué suplicio baña la frente el silencio / Detrás de la ausencia mirabas sin fuego / Es ausencia noche / Pero los ojos el fuego / Caricia estío los ojos la boca / El fuego nace en los ojos / El amor nace en los ojos el cielo el fuego / El fuego el amor el silencio]

Some thirty years ago, before retiring into the provinces and private life, I was a student of Eric Mottram. As a teacher, he seemed at first difficult and fiery, and yet so manifestly in earnest and without teacherly tricks, that it was worth my while to wrestle with my ignorance in order to understand. I soon came to honour him for the honesty, relevance and sheer intellectual speed and drive of his lectures. He never talked down, ignored the possibility that some of his audience might not be seriously interested, and opened up the world of American literature. Later, I learned a little of his knowledge of music (jazz, classical, romantic and twentieth-century), and his pioneering response to major poets of our time, British and American. I remember also his kindness and hospitality to the gauche and jejune, his generosity in kind and time.

Quite recently, after a quarter of a century, our friendship was renewed. Eric was, incredibly, retiring. How could a force of nature, an intellectual furnace, retire? By now I had read some of his poetry and realised how far he had travelled, how much he had made, during our twenty-five year gap.

When we met, I found that what I'd forgotten was his kindness and openness, and a certain gentleness behind the seeming ferocity. He hadn't tired or slowed down as far as I could see (in fact, he still hasn't). Operating as he does on the cusp of form-as-meaning, he has a fierce contempt for the merely trendy as opposed to the genuinely new. He is still moving on, restlessly ahead of us, investigating, exploring, risking, recording and making. But the same openness, the same warmth is still there, and one suddenly remembers that this is the man who once passed the time of day with a bear. Eric says he thought it was a tramp, but I'm not so sure. At all events, there he was, relating to the world, the other, in a social way. Naval war veteran, one time guest of Hopi Indians, scholar, critic, teacher and poet, Eric Mottram is internationally known and admired. In these drear times, we need him and his work more than ever. His friendship is an enduring resource. Salve, magister. Gratias tibi ago.

JOAN STEEN WILENTZ, For Eric's Birthday

The smile, the red cheeks, the scarf flying in the wind... the images of Eric that come to mind are of the man in motion, talking fast, the ideas tumbling over each other, colliding and bouncing apart... a thought gives rise to a name, to a book, to a reference, a connection not previously considered. All this while walking from NYU or the subway or over tea or drinks or dinner.

I first met Eric not long after I married Ted Wilentz and Eric was in America on one of his several tours of duty as guest lecturer, researcher, worthy recipient of funding from this or that learned society or university. He brought presents, useful and pretty – a copper pitcher – an earthenware crock to cook fish in – and for dinner a favorite Portuguese wine to drink.

I remember conversations and debates: about film, rock music, happenings, the Beats, the Beatles, the Fugs; who and what was new... Is photography derivative or a true art form? (Several martinis to resolve that one.) About Tinguely and Nam June Paik and Amiri Baraka. At one point I was involved in a psychology text project that triggered discussions on the nature of man and human nature... on the origins of religion, cosmology myths, Levi-Strauss, the commonalities across cultures... and long reading lists of "you really ought to look at...

We named our second son's second name after Eric, whose method of meeting and greeting his namesake was to pick him up and swing him round, exhibiting centrifugal forces and Dervish whirls, delighting the small one; winding the big one. With the years the postcards would come from holidays in Wales with maps and pictures of trains.

Then there is the music. I remember when Eric was still living in his basement flat when he played Mozart for me one afternoon, lovely and quietly. As in so many areas Eric's taste and knowledge is profound and wide: Mozart and Berlioz and Frank Martin and John Cage; old jazz and new jazz; what's new; what's good.

Finally, food. Eric the host serves up Eric specialities more likely to have derived from stints abroad than home. Eric the guest is the charming conversationalist ready to engage in comfortable patter or serious colloquies – and on occasion hysterical exchanges – like the time when he and an English-cum-Canadian woman friend of ours spent the better part of a meal out-doing each other in English maxims – everything from a stitch in time saves nine to putting a beggar on the gentleman...

And in that vein let us say, "Hats off!" and "Three cheers". Hail Mottram, Mottram rules the waves... and continents of culture. We love you dearly and wish you a whale of a birthday and many long, prosperous, and productive years ahead.

Basil Bunting, Eric Mottram, Barbara De Loach, Allen De Loach; at the De Loachs' apartment, Chapel Road, Buffalo NY, July 1966. Photograph by Allen De Loach

Eric Mottram in his Vicarage Gate flat, London, 1960s. Photographer not known.

My association with Professor Mottram is as a witness defending *Last Exit To Brooklyn*. Naturally I am grateful to him for all his efforts on behalf of the book, but my appreciation goes much beyond this. His contribution as an expert witness during the trial was of great value, but I believe we all owe him a vote, and debt, of gratitude for defending artistic freedom and integrity. There are always those who will attack this freedom as they are terrified at the mere thought that people have the inalienable right to *think* a thought other than those they would permit, and the same right to express those thoughts. There is nothing more terrifying to these people than an *idea* because they know the power it has.

So, as I perceive it, Professor Mottram was defending not only a book, but the symbol of freedom it represents. There have always existed many forms of tyranny, and in order for a tyrant to succeed he must do everything possible to prevent the free and open exchange of *ideas*. This, it seems to me, is the foundation of all tyranny. Professor Mottram not only defended the right of free people to read this book, but their right to freedom from all forms of tyranny.

HAPPY BIRTHDAY ERIC! and I hope this day finds you well and happy and enjoying the Blessings of Life.

JEROME ROTHENBERG, Sea Thoughts, After Apollinaire

For Eric at seventy

Oh voice I speak the language of the sea

1

when I saw that line – was it Apollinaire's? – I told them
poets have always written about the sea
have loved it for its depths
& for the salt that echoes memory –
in blackness it is black –
in whiteness like a distant light,
whiter than drowning

2

lost on its path the ocean
no longer the platform for recovery
the place where you & I wait
& listen to its language   its words in waves
the sea like a dark canyon
that pulls us,
down or forever downward
not to drown (though drowning beckons)
but to recover a lost nerve
& swim, orphan to danger
back to where the sky has settled over us
bright as your eye

3

sea *is* language   & we spell
with globulets
we speak with sand over our cheeks
the trickledown so fine
we drown from it
as she did, mother, long ago
the memory that far behind us
awaits us in a distant port
o china sky o sacred city
let me turn back from you & swim
a little further out

We first met in the summer of '66 in Leslie Fiedler's garden at his annual 4th of July party in Buffalo.

In the years 1969-72, when I was teaching at University College, Aberystwyth, Eric served as our External Examiner. At that time, it was considered that only someone of professorial standing would be an External. Even then, Eric was clearly the most knowledgeable American Literature and Cultural Studies man in Britain. The fact that he had achieved only the grade of Lecturer at King's was a scandal in the world of British higher education. Of course, it was to be expected, since Eric was a committed educator, a committed socialist, and his literary preferences were not exactly ever going to endear him to the established forces of clout.

I remember how he, in formal meetings, was clearly "on the students' side" in terms of advocacy; yet, he balanced that with insistence on consistently high standards. He was almost evangelical in his peregrinations throughout the island in the cause of quality teaching and imaginative degree programs.

That same demand for high standards scorched the souls of the cozy old-boy network not only in Academe, but also in the poetry world when he became Editor of POETRY REVIEW. Attacked almost from the start, he managed to put out the twenty issues of POETRY REVIEW which are arguably the finest five years of editing of a poetry quarterly in the long history of such enterprises.

Of course, one is not objective here, since in his capacity as Editor of POETRY REVIEW Eric championed my own work time and again, giving me the confidence I needed.

We came to meet often during those South London days throughout the 1970s. When I was struggling with the painful dissolution of my marriage to an Englishwoman, Eric was always there to offer a discourse of ideas, and ideas in action, which helped me to survive, and not simply to displace my sorrow, but to sublimate it, and deal with it.

One day on the phone Eric put me onto Gwyn A. Williams's footnote on the John Evans materials in Seville, and so made possible the composition of *Spanish Songs in Mandaine Land.*

Almost two years after my first myocardial, I returned to my native Philadelphia in 1982, and Eric and I saw each other mainly during those occasions each year when I found myself back in Britain. Now, each time I come to London, I look forward to seeing my old friend again, and to being delighted by his sense of humour and the pleasure of his company. And his gourmet cooking!

"I lit my fire
    I greased my skillet
        And I cooked"

The Bird was on the wing
    before his now's the time to come
        drifting on the hardest reed

Looked east down Broadway
    saw Allah in the rising sun
        in the spaces in between

Ate the petals of the rose
    the dial set clear
        abstracted the body of music

Alone on the stand at Birdland
    the caged finches, the silver pigeon
        the midget in the white suit

Flung his garment of repentance
    laughed at the juggler
        the bricks flying in the air

Six pretty horses

"Crazy"

LESLIE FIEDLER

During 1967-68, the only time I have taught in England, I never ceased feeling a stranger in a strange land. Though I had been invited by the University of Sussex to give courses in American literature and culture —and though my academic colleagues were scrupulously congenial and polite— I never had the sense that they and I spoke the same language, much less dreamed the same dreams. To be sure, many of the American books which were the source of those dreams were assigned reading for the students in my charge. I felt, however, as if I had not merely to explicate them but, as it were, to translate them to make them available. This was even more spectacularly the case with faculty members throughout England, heirs to a tradition of snobbism and condescension toward our culture, which they were therefore proud to misunderstand.

In light of all this, you can imagine with what gratification and relief I encountered Eric Mottram. English to the core, he yet understood what our classic books, those earliest products of the first self-conscious post-colonial culture, really were as well as were not. Moreover, he was aware of how in the post-modern era, even as the Pop Culture of that former British colony was becoming the Pop Culture of the entire world, the line between it and High Art was blurring to indistinction. These insights he was able to expound to his less savvy compatriots with the wit and grace appropriate to one who was a poet as well as a critic.

I have been pleased in the years since to discover how many younger scholars (on my side of the Atlantic as well as his) have been influenced by him. Yes in retrospect I am dismayed by how slowly and reluctantly his older colleagues have come to recognize his unique gifts —only belatedly granting him the full academic status he deserved early on.

It has, in any case, been a source of delight to me that I have continued to meet and converse with him in both our countries: a delight compounded by the opportunity to help honor him properly at long last.

ELAINE FEINSTEIN, Eric Mottram

Some time in 1968, when I was living in Brighton, the poet Bill Butler, who ran a bookshop there, was charged with the sale of pornographic books. I was to be a witness for the defence, and a box of books – including, I remember, Ginsberg's *Howl,* a run of EVERGREEN REVIEW and a pamphlet of J.G. Ballard's *Why I Want to Fuck Ronald Reagan* – arrived at my house. Soon afterwards, I made the acquaintance of Eric Mottram, a stocky, pugnacious figure in a white polo neck shirt, navy blazer and flannels, who had come down from London University to do battle on behalf of the avant garde.

It is a battle Eric has always continued to fight. He loved the whole network of Black Mountain poets at a time when there were very few enthusiasts in Great Britain. He was part of that astonishing mimeographic revolution which enabled poets to bypass commercial publishing, and he took a particular delight in introducing to one another the sometimes articulate, sometimes hesitant, creatures of that underworld. Wherever he gave his allegiance, he was loyal and generous. And he cared about prose as well as poetry. I don't think any other friend read my early novels with such attention care, or wrote such detailed letters to me about them.

There was a clutch of English poets for whom we shared an admiration; but we didn't always agree, and he wouldn't want me to pretend we did. I still feel an enormous gratitude towards him for all the knowledge and help ' he offered me when I first began writing. It is very doubtful whether there is any comparable presence in the literary world of today.

Facing page: **PAULA CLAIRE,** Bemused, a participation text for voices and instruments, 22.6.94.
For Eric Mottram

use us
use us
use us
use us
use us
use us
use us
use us
use us

muse
    muse
  be   muse
    be   be muse
  muse   be   muse   muse
    BE muse   be   muse   muse   use us
        mUSe   be   use us
  BE   mUSe   mUSEmUSe
      BE   BEMUSE muse use us muse
                    use us   be muse
                                muse be muse
                    use us   muse MUSE be be muse
        MUSIC   music   music use   mUSE   be   be muse
      MUSICMUSICMUSICMUSE   be   be mUSe
                use us music   musicmusic mUSe muse
                use us   mUSe muse
                        mUSe   mUSe use us   mUSE
          muse   mUSE   be   BE muse USE US muse mUSE
    MUSE   be   BE   muse
    muse   museBE   BE   mUSe muse muse use us
  be   BE BE   mUSe muse   use us
    be MUSE mUSE muse   use us
muse   use us
                               use us
                               use us
                               use us
                               use us
                               use us
                               use us
                               use us
                               use us
                               use us
                               use us
                               use us
                               use us
                               use us
                               use us
                               use us
                               use us
                               use us
                               use us
                               use us
                               use us
                               use us
                               use us

when night tips over into day
here I am and there you are
separate but speaking across
the space that separates us
dawn is a time to begin again
with words and clusters of words
looks, acts, omissions, gestures
to define, deny and redefine
a complex, changing space
it is a world in common
heavy traffic grates on the bend
and yet a new configuration
of common words or gestures
can place everything at risk

I was eighteen years old, a raw undergraduate at King's College London. Milling around with twenty or thirty others mostly unknown to me in one of those many brown inaccessible rooms in which the old King's building abounded (still abounds) (you needed a degree to work out how to find them sometimes), waiting for the first lecture in the American Literature option I'd chosen, I heard this booming guffaw from the back of the room. What was that? *That* was Eric Mottram (not yet Professor).

Minutes later he stepped up to the podium and the lecture began, at high speed. My biro flew over my pristine ruled pad but could scarcely keep up. "The linear novel is finished" is one of the first things I remember him saying. I wrote it down though I didn't really know what it meant. He was wrong and he was right. Even today the linear novel is very much still with us. But perhaps it ought to be finished.

Twenty-five years later I count Eric as a good friend. And an important influence on my subsequent development as a writer and poet. He was the first to tell me the best poets in England at the time were Lee Harwood and Tom Raworth, of whom I had never heard (I thought Ted Hughes daringly modern then). Of course I immediately went looking for their books.

But that's not an unusual story. How many contributors to this book will have similar tales to tell? And many others too. For example, some time ago reading the late Derek Jarman's first autobiography *Dancing Ledge* I came across this: "through my tutor Eric Mottram I discovered the existence of Allen Ginsberg and William Burroughs" (it's virtually the only reference Jarman makes in his writing to *his* three years as an undergraduate at King's in the early Sixties).

For this collection, I initially wrote a formal sonnet to Eric, obeying all the standard rules (the first time I'd done anything of the sort since my teenage years). I thought it would be amusing. Then I thought he wouldn't be so amused. Not because the poem was slightly rude, but because of the iambics – and the personal nature of the address. "That personal stuff" as he disparagingly dubs much lyric poetry, including some of my own.

So instead I append the beginning of a draft of a long poem I am still working on, which explores among other things the Mediterranean origins of my family. The reason for this choice being that it makes use of Braudel's immense work on the Mediterranean which (of course) Eric brought to my attention. The poem when finished will be dedicated to Eric, but please be aware that the "you" in it is not he but I.

Bird Migration In The 21st Century

1

Some time in the era of great light
Began the history of the future
A whole-body music whose complexity & strangeness
Shape-changed in the DNA mix twisting
In the thermals of the centuries
                                    In later years she was to remember
The time of the evacuation
Genoese
Naval officers, stationed in the zone at the Maghrib's apex
Fascisti boys unknowing laughing
                        Pioneers
Of international capital

2

I'd have thought you could learn something from it
But the more spread out the object I suppose
The harder it is to handle

Spread through history spread through the gene pool
A ripple of mistakes creates the new
The one coming off the other over & over unspiralling
But ignorance confused
What can be changed with what's beyond attainment
The movement's this:
From gold silver & copper
                        to paper
                                    to digital information
Encoded in the data streams that flow
From terminal to terminal along the ancient trade routes

3

Or as the White Stork and Honey Buzzard
Take the eastern or the western paths from northern Europe
To sub-Saharan Africa & back
Two hundred thousand raptors & storks a year
On the thermals over Gibraltar Straits

4

Its constant & inconstant flow, its periods humanly ungraspable
Which was her blood & yours
As fortunes thrived stagnated or declined — Genoese
To Catalonia in the lateen rig, yet hugging the coasts for fear
Refusing the lodestone —
You knew only family, that was fear

Salt cheese iron money & capital
A relatively modest wealth to take from shortage, pass down the generations
Coral
Water-celery crystallised in sugar
Buntings in barrels pickled in vinegar
The Cyprus tree which flowers in clusters like the vine
Whose distilled leaves produce the orange dye
Used to colour the tails of gentlemen's horses

5

At breakfast
I see her familiar russet brown back flash
The female kestrel has returned
To search on Peckham Rye common for rodents
No 12 goes past
No 78 stands by
The girl in the patchwork coat is walking her brisk dog

CLIVE BUSH, poet in a company of musicians

for Eric Mottram

I

not by the child only
        a way comes through
the malice

break it down
        go to
the wall of stone

it is not in the grand effect
        but in
lucid oppositions of tone

that an impulse lifts
        effective
for grief

you would need
        rather to starve
than do what they do

by ear
        the whole body
bears witness to this

    ***

seven days and a spiral
        I shouted
his name

it rang in
        on Max Ernst's soul
from the preparation of the rock

it was as if I had died
        and heard my name
in a new world

I have cleaned house
　　　what is left
is on the clothes line

II

je ne suis pas aisé
　　　if it was left to publishers
Bach would not appear

harmony
　　　placed off limits
forgets the chord of nature

no flood
　　　of
fragmented pieces

lights a motion of surface on water
　　　where curls fall
the whirling rises

the living anachronism
　　　is not the pastiche
laboured

in the absence of God
　　　nothing changes
only the timbre shifts

a ruined river
　　　takes two saxophones
but one and a trombone would do it

säume, letztes Licht
　　　jetzt speist mein Geist Honig
aus des Löwen Munde

playing I am gone
I am sound
I am process

je suis comme un samovar
je fume par les narines
comme dans Wagner

who will measure time
      by music
shines the note of the child

Marshall McLuhan and I share boyhood memories centred about Gertrude Avenue between the Red and Assiniboine Rivers in Winnipeg, Manitoba, "where children played baseball on the street, using a sewer cover as home plate and boulevard trees as first and third bases". We both admired the nearby firehall and attended Gladstone Public School where McLuhan failed Grade 6 and I failed Grade 1, but found nothing alarming in that. And so we grew up, nostalgic about home, and aware of a spotty education. "One advantage we Westerners have is that we're under no illusions we've had an education" (Philip Marchand, *Marshall McLuhan: The Medium and the Messenger* Toronto, 1989). This was Marshall McLuhan's explanation for his seeking out Cambridge after his graduate degree from the University of Manitoba. It reflects the Western Canadian's cultural insecurity, the Young Man from the Provinces' need for wider experience. What he found in Cambridge was far beyond what he could have hoped for. Through the new, literary critical analysis of I.A. Richards and William Empson and, more especially, through F.R. Leavis's application of these critical precepts to the social environment in such works as *Culture and Environment* (1933), McLuhan discovered his life's work.

How does one find what one needs even when one hasn't a clue what that might be? How does one land in the very place that might provide it? McLuhan's remarkable luck in his search for an education reflects my own happy stumbling off the Strand into King's College and into the presence of Eric Mottram.

What struck *this* boy from the provinces was not the supposed dazzling elegance of British academia, a colonial fantasy, but the deeply searching analyses of cultural history and the superb, synthesizing imagination exemplified in Eric Mottram's lectures and writings. Here were techniques of analysis that recognized complexity and refused simple, linear explanations. Here was the beginning of serious education remote from the careerist strategies and literary games that often passed for graduate study.

I learned that, with Mottram, one's studies could be exploratory but, like surgery, they had to be precise and informed. Long ago, Mottram resisted the notion that English Studies were somehow the soft-centre in the university box of chocolates, arguing that English was "a discipline as involving and strenuous as biochemistry or architecture" (TIMES LITERARY SUPPLEMENT, Dec. 3, 1964). Mottram believes, with Thoreau, that reading is "a noble exercise, and one that will task the reader more than any exercise which the customs of the day esteem. It requires a training such as athletes underwent..." (*Walden*, Ch. 3). And Mottram, like Whitman, is "the teacher of athletes".

In Mottram, one also found a man whose training in cultural studies was, like Marshal McLuhan's, Cambridge based and, it turned out, importantly influenced by his own encounter with McLuhan. The language of probes, multiple environments, total field situations and the search for procedures to handle information mark Mottram's regard for McLuhan's work. Both men appreciate the student's sense of urgency in acquiring techniques for coping with life in this century. Both are aware of the disastrous consequences of a bad education and take Poe's "A Descent into The Maelstrom" as a cautionary tale where understanding works against victimization. Caught in the maelstrom, the man "staved off disaster by understanding the action of the whirlpool" (McLuhan, *The Medium is the Message*). Just as Twain's learning the fixed signs and laws required of a riverboat pilot was good training for a writer, so Mottram's training as a naval officer on a minesweeper looks like an appropriate preparation for an alert and wary survivor/cultural critic in a hostile environment.

In London, then, the prairie boy learned to swim or to paddle or, at least, how not to sink full fathom five. He owed something to his countryman who shared that leafy street between two rivers. He owed much to the buoyant teaching of the former sweeper of mines.

Facing page: **R.B. KITAJ,** Robert Duncan
Love from Kitaj to Eric

I love Eric Mottram because he makes me look and listen carefully where I would not have done so before. Strangely enough all the other great Erics in history have done the same; Eric Bloodaxe, Eric the Red, Eric Morecambe and Eric Burdon. In old Irish law a fine paid by a murderer to the family of a victim was called an eric. The trouble is there has never been enough of them to go around. This is a fuck poem written in honour of the old Eric.

Hidden Agenda

I want to be an astronaut of fuck
to be flung into orbit around fuck

I want to be the oil in the engine of fuck
turbocharged with the rocket fuel of fuck
I want to spin on the pinnacle of fuck
I want to absorb fuck through my pores

I want to be swept into fuck
wrapped in fuck
swallowed in fuck
foaming in fuck
free in fuck
fast in fuck
fixed in fuck
loved in fuck

I want accommodation in fuck
security of tenure in fuck
I want to dive in fuck
swim sink and drown in fuck
I want to be re-born in fuck
and die in fuck

I want a daily delivery of fuck
an early morning milk round of fuck
I want to duck diet and dissolve in fuck
I want to dream in fuck

I want to fuck about with fuck
float in fuck shout in fuck
dance in fuck
sing in fuck

I want fuck to pour down on me
I want cloud bursts of fuck
and heat-waves of fuck
I want torrents of fuck
swamps blizzards tornadoes
and earthquakes of fuck
volcanoes of fuck
floods of fuck
I want to be deluged in fuck
immersed and inundated in fuck

I want flash floods of fuck
waves of fuck
tides of fuck
I want tidal waves of fuck
torrents streams and lakes of fuck
I want to turn on the tap and fill the bath with fuck
I want to be tossed in a force eight gale of fuck

I want fuck falling out of trees
I want fuck dispensed on the hour every hour
I want to be glutted with buckets of global fuck
inter planetary inter galactic and colliding galaxies of fuck
I want black holes of fuck
forests of fuck
shoals of fuck
showers of fuck

I want cities built on fuck
fermenting fuck
farms of fuck
fields flowering fuck
I want to be lost in the Bermuda triangle of fuck

I want to be sucked in fuck
tucked in fuck
dipped in fuck
I want to lick fuck
and drip fuck
I want fuck sent to me by special delivery
I want fuck to come by first class post
and fuck for the foreseeable future

I want to be baptised in the font of fuck
to get familiar with the fundamentals of fuck
to become ordained in the order of fuck

I want to travel daily on a fuck bus
to excavate the mines of fuck
I want to feast in the kitchens of fuck
and be basted on the spit of fuck
to kneel and be knighted by the queen of fuck
arise Sir Thomas Fuckard and kiss my quim

I want to live in the welfare state of the republic of fuck
I want fuck back on the national curriculum

I want to take fuck by her scruffy neck
and rub my face in the nub of fuck

WOLFGANG GÖRTSCHACHER, Inside the Whale of Britain's Literary Establishment

After an interregnum of six months, when two issues of POETRY REVIEW were guest-edited, Eric Mottram was elected to the editorship of the Poetry Society's organ in 1971. His election was initiated by internal reforms within the Poetry Society in the late 'sixties and early 'seventies. Stuart Montgomery, then Chairman of the Association of Little Presses (ALP), and Bob Cobbing, the Secretary of ALP, were elected to the Poetry Society's Council in 1967 and 1968 respectively. At the first Poets' Conference held in July 1970 poets were urged to join the Poetry Society in an attempt to make their influence felt.

To quote a Poets' Conference "State of Poetry" supplement:

> By 1974, there had been elected to the Council a majority of poets and others active in the cause of reform. They implemented a policy of opening The Poetry Society to the public and to poets. A printshop in the basement was begun and expanded to help poets publish their work cheaply and simply, together with a small bookshop to aid distribution. New workshops and weekend events were commenced, with regular exhibitions and book fairs, and a greatly expanded series of lectures and readings. An archive of poetry on tape and record was begun, and an attempt to modernise The Poetry Society's library. The Society was open five nights a week at least, and the printshop, voluntarily supervised, often in use seven days a week.

> This policy met instant opposition: from the paid staff who resented the extra work; from conservatives on the Council who objected to the concept of poetry moving forwards and outwards; and from Charles Osborne who saw all this as a threat to his own control of the poetry world and the narrow establishment policy he wished to pursue.[1]

Barry MacSweeney of Blacksuede Boot Press, Chairman of the Poetry Society's Council from 1976 to 1977, described the new atmosphere at 21 Earl's Court Square: "poets found a central forum to discuss and read work on a regular basis, to talk about the effects of the English tradition on their own work. The society became a lively home."[2] The poets' reactions, however, were diverse and far from uniform, culminating in various disputes, e.g., between Ian Robinson of OASIS and William Oxley of LITTACK in TRIBUNE in 1976. Whereas the former held that "anything new and vital is bound to upset those whose tastes are rooted in the past"[3] and that the present somehow nullifies the past, Oxley voiced what MacSweeney would have considered, at that time, a "reactionary and narrow"[4] view against the tenets of the Poetry Society:

> poetry, as well as art, being an individual craft, is not amenable to being organised. Organise it and you kill it. Make it the subject of committees, and you organise its death slowly. Any institution is bound to become a funeral for the art that it presumes to promote.[5]

Mottram projected the magazine into what he regarded as the British Poetry Revival – "the fact that our poetry has again reached a stage of fine quality and extraordinary range"[6] – throwing his readership in at the deep end of international experimental poetry. He tried to publish a wide range of British poetry and made a wider public familiar with American avant-garde poetry. The exponents of the alternative strand in the British Poetry Revival emphasised the oral, spoken, performance component of poetry rather than its visual, page-only, written dimension, experimenting with the various potentialities of audience involvement, mixing the various art forms with poetry, "involving spoken poetry with jazz, plays, mime, new music, electronics, speeches, film, light/sound projections, sculpture, dance."[7] They were characterised by an explicit openness to international, in particular American, influences, and availed themselves of a wide range of experimental forms and avant-garde techniques, i.e., conceptual forms, typewriter poetry, cut-up methods, concrete, surrealist, dada lyric, open field, sound text, found texts, collages, mail-art, dream poems, etc. In fact, this innovative poetry relies on the synthesis of these poetic forms encountered in, and derived from, various international poetries, which is why it defies any rigid categorization.

Mottram also put great emphasis on poetry in translation by publishing work by Peter Handke, Helmut Heissenbüttel, Peter Huchel, Ernst Jandl, Sarah Kirsch (all translated by Michael Hamburger), Tristan Corbiere (trans. Val Warner) and Michel Deguy (trans. Anthony Rudolf). "In the event British and American poetry dominated; the weakness in POETRY REVIEW was certainly in the relative absence of adequate translations from continental Europe and Latin America."[8] Mottram certainly managed to inject new life into what had been a rather stale magazine with a very narrow range of interests. POETRY REVIEW was brought up to date and, by giving up its parochialism, became a review whose internationalism was limited to America, France and Germany. During his six years' term Mottram edited twenty numbers, printing work from more than 200 Continental, American and British poets. In 1971 Mottram set out with the plan "to publish as wide a range as possible of the new British poetry, the best of American poetry, and whatever could be managed from translation."[9]

From 62.3 (Autumn 1971) to 65.2-3 (Autumn 1974) Mottram considered it necessary to print listings of recent publications under the heading "Poetry Information", which was divided into the sections "Contributors", "Recent British Poetry", "Recent American Poetry", "Concrete and Sound Poetry", "Translations", "Bibliographical and Critical Anthologies", "Recent Magazines", "Sound Poetry Records", and "Poetry Society Section". From the above headings one can immediately recognize the editor's catholic editorial policy, which was, nevertheless, described by more conservative circles as "weird oscillations of taste"[10] and his contributors as an anti-establishment clique who only substituted for the old establishment. Peter Finch, who was elected to the Poetry Society's General Council in 1972, provides a quasi-eyewitness account of the reception Mottram's first issue received from its traditionally-oriented readers: "the poetry society ladies were aghast, ex-majors handed their resignations in, traditional english gentlemen choked over their toast and jam. this is not poetry!"[sic].[11] From A to Z the poets printed in POETRY REVIEW ranged from Jeremy Adler, who ran Alphabox Press, to Franz Wurm in Hamburger's rendering, including, among others, the New York and Black Mountain poets, the Cambridge group (Peter Riley, John James, Andrew Crozier), Bob Cobbing, Peter Finch, Ian Hamilton Finlay, Roy and Allen Fisher, Bill Griffiths, Tom Pickard, F.T. Prince, Carl Rakosi, Ken Smith, Chris Torrance, and many others. From 65.4 onwards readers were referred to the listings printed in POETRY INFORMATION edited by Peter Hodgkiss. Artistic covers, designed by poets, such as Jeff Nuttall, Peter Finch, Bob Cobbing and Ian Hamilton Finlay, replaced the sterile cover of earlier years.

POETRY REVIEW's target group were not those who consumed poetry as a leisure pastime but the poets themselves. "This meant, of course, that it ran against the grain of contemporary British culture, in which the arts are taken by the rulers and their middle class administrators to be purely the prerogative of the consumer in the marketplace."[12] Mottram's reforms created such a stir that the magazine hit the headlines of the national newspapers. Taking on Mottram at the end of his editorship, Douglas Dunn criticised this supposed "outpost of American and European modernism" for having substituted an elite à la experiment for experiment's sake for what MacSweeney termed "reactionaries" and "a minor coterie of so-called intellectual adherents":

> their publicity, their activities, their attitudes give the unmistakable impression that the outpost is larger than the main citadel, that the wrong and imitative are right, and that those with the strength of mind not to copy William Carlos Williams, Tristan Tzara – or anyone else for that matter – simply don't know where it's at.[13]

Mottram relied always on building each issue around work which had been specifically commissioned. That is why only very few unknown poets - an exception was Bill Griffiths, who supported Mottram in the mid-'seventies – had their work printed in POETRY REVIEW. Mottram wanted the magazine to act as a selective focus for what he regarded as a major British poetry revival. As the editor of POETRY REVIEW, which more and more became, according to Booth, "a kind of central axis around which both establishment and fringe and small magazine publications revolved or evolved"[14], Mottram could draw "on an abundance of excellent poetry journals and small independent press publications"[15].

Mottram opposed, in a straightforward attack, views held by Establishment critics, like Anthony Thwaite's in THE LISTENER in 1973, that there are just two poetries in the UK: one believes in "shape, form, [and] control" (Fuller, Larkin, Hamilton), the other in "spontaneity, immediacy, and energy released by both poet and audience in an instant flash of communion" (Ginsberg, Horovitz, Nuttall, Patten).[16] In sharp contrast to Thwaite's opinion that Ginsberg's *Reality Sandwiches* "reveals all its facets and depths and resonances at a single reading or hearing", Mottram maintained that the new experimental poetry of the 'sixties, unlike the officially sanctioned British poetry, "went beyond a leisure-hour consumer's inclination to rapid reading". It was not written "for the middle-class rapid-reader looking for instant significance, or alibis in established culture."[17]

On 26th March 1977 fourteen poets and editors – Barry MacSweeney, Peter Hodgkiss, Jeremy Adler, Peter Finch, Bill Griffiths, Cris Cheek, Lawrence Upton, Allen Fisher, Bob Cobbing, Jeff Nuttall, Tom Pickard, Pete Morgan, Ian Patterson and Ken Smith – resigned from the General Council after the Poetry Society had adopted the Witt Report, which recommended Arts Council "control through an effective Assessorship carried out by the Literature Director"[18]. In a press release they concluded that "The Council is no longer in control of Society policy. Policy is being controlled by the Arts Council of Great Britain and the Society's paid staff.[19] Charles Osborne maintained that he had, by mere coincidence, initiated the investigation. The Arts Council directly intervened to dissolve POETRY REVIEW's editorial board, which put an end to Mottram's policy of featuring international, modernist, experimental work. These developments at the Poetry Society marked a decisive turning-point in what Mottram termed the British Poetry Revival, i.e., the popularisation of (post-) modernist, experimental poetry and put an end to one of the most long-lived editorships of POETRY REVIEW after 1945 and, in R.J. Ellis's view, "a remarkable period in the review's long history"[20].

The Arts Council immediately swung the pendulum the other way and turned down applications for grant-aid, which might have been accepted in 1976. The avant-garde small presses and little magazines that were refused further grant-aid included Writers Forum (for KROKLOK MAGAZINE and books by Mottram, Themerson, Houédard and Cobbing), Aloes Books (for

Pickard, MacSweeney and Griffiths), SPANNER, Arc Publications, Albion Village, Trigram and POETRY INFORMATION.

Mottram's assessment that the literary Establishment's rigidity and closed-shop policy is still prevalent has proved to be, over the years, rather perceptive. Thwaite's view and Blake Morrison and Andrew Motion's debunking remark that the 'sixties and 'seventies were "a spell of lethargy [...] when very little – in England at any rate – seemed to be happening"[21] are tenets still widely accepted among literary critics and academics. Concerning the big presses' closed-shop policy, Paladin, an imprint of Harper Collins Publishers, has, with its recent publications of modernist poetry, initiated what could well develop into an undermining of the rigid closed canon of mainstream presses.

In the anthology *The New British Poetry*, published by Paladin in 1988, Mottram once again hit back at the Arts Council of (not only) 1977, which regarded the inclusion of 'foreign poets' as "a treacherous assault on British poetry"[22], by printing recent work of twenty-five poets who began writing in the British Poetry Revival of the 'sixties and early 'seventies and all of whom, with the exception of two, he published in POETRY REVIEW between 1971 and 1977. The most widely known poets represented in this overdue anthology section, which is in itself an updated POETRY REVIEW-issue of the 'seventies, still edited with a modernist stance, are Cobbing, Crozier, Roy Fisher, Griffiths, Harwood, MacSweeney, Jeff Nuttall, Tom Pickard, Raworth, Ken Smith and Gael Turnbull. Mottram describes the poets of the British Poetry Revival as "explorers in language and form" and "internationalists who nevertheless live and work in the variety of British culture [and] belong to no enclosure of school or movement". These poets who have, in the majority of cases, been neglected by official histories of 20th-century British poetry are assigned their adequate place when Mottram concludingly maintains:

> What remains from that period, and continues, is a legacy of creative innovation that has thrown up a number of important poets, encouraged younger writers, and taken as a whole, constitutes one of the finest and most challenging poetries in the world today.[23]

NOTES: [1] Quoted in Bill Griffiths and Bob Cobbing (eds.): *ALP: The First 22 ¹/₂ Years. A Palpi Supplement.* London: ALP, 1988: 13. Mottram himself provides his readers with firsthand information on the Poetry Society and his editorship of POETRY REVIEW in an interview with Peterjon Skelt published in *Prospect Into Breath: Interviews with North and South Writers.* Ed. Peterjon Skelt. Twickenham: North and South, 1991: 13-42. [2] Barry MacSweeney: "The British Poetry Revival 1965-1979". SOUTH EAST ARTS REVIEW (Spring 1979): 34. [3] Ian Robinson: "Letter". TRIBUNE, 30 April

1976: 10. [4] B. MacSweeney: "The British Poetry Revival 1965-1979": 44. [5] William Oxley: "Organise Poetry and You Kill It". TRIBUNE, 14 May 1976: 10. [6] Eric Mottram: "The British Poetry Revival 1960-1974". Modern British Poetry Conference 1974. London: The Polytechnic of Central London, 1974: 86. Mottram coined the phrase "The British Poetry Revival" in this essay. It was taken up by Barry MacSweeney in his essay "The British Poetry Revival 1965-1979". [7] Michael Horovitz: "Afterwords". *Children of Albion.* Harmondsworth: Penguin, 1969: 321. [8] E. Mottram: "Editing POETRY REVIEW". POETRY INFORMATION 20-21 (Winter 1979/80): 154. [9] Ibid.: 154. [10] Neil Corcoran: "The Periodicals, 6: POETRY REVIEW", TIMES LITERARY SUPPLEMENT, 4 Nov. 1983: 1219. [11] Peter Finch: "The UK Scene". MARGINS 8 (Oct.-Nov. 1973): 33. [12] E. Mottram: "Editing POETRY REVIEW": 154. [13] Douglas Dunn: "Coteries & Commitments: Little Magazines". ENCOUNTER 48.6 (June 1977): 62. [14] Martin Booth: *British Poetry 1964-84: Driving through the Barricades.* London, Boston, Melbourne, et al: Routledge & Kegan Paul, 1985: 70. [15] E. Mottram: "A Treacherous Assault on British Poetry". *The New British Poetry.* Ed. Gillian Allnutt, Fred D'Aguiar, Ken Edwards, Eric Mottram. London, Glasgow, Toronto, et al.: Paladin, 1988: 132. [16] Anthony Thwaite: "The Two Poetries". THE LISTENER, 5 April 1973: 452. [17] E. Mottram: "The British Poetry Revival 1960-1974": 87. [18] Quoted in *ALP: The First 22 1/2 Years:* 13. [19] Ibid.: 13. [20] R.J. Ellis: "Producing the Poem: UK Little Magazines – A Second Survey (Part 1)". SERIALS REVIEW (Winter 1984): 16. An index of all the issues edited by Mottram was published in POETRY INFORMATION 20-21 (Winter 1979/80): 142-155. [21] Blake Morrison and Andrew Motion (eds.): "Introduction". *Contemporary British Poetry.* London: Penguin, 1982: 11. [22] E. Mottram: "A Treacherous Assault on British Poetry": 133. [23] Ibid.: 132-133.

RICHARD CUPIDI, ViVa!

Dear Eric,

& after all these years
I have never ceased wondering
how you –

fight the good poetry wars
wordsmith at an alarming rate
lock Hernes with just about everyone
rebore General Motors
biograph the good & great
champion the word as if text mattered
teach
talk Apollo and spit Dionysus
inspire dedication in a posse of students
reformulate the American Books of the Dead
                 & nearly Dead

& still manage to laugh
like a demented pixie??

affectionately yours,

Richard Cupidi

ELAINE RANDELL, The Other Absolute

"Time is the other absolute.
Time is crucial to mapping the
heavens: we do not know in the
first place how far away stars are,
only at what moment they pass
across our line of sight.
So the mariners world called
for the perfection of two sets
of instruments – clocks and telescope,
the poet called for
intuition and song"
This hints at greater ideas,
experienced horror, love, loss,
belief, suffering and recovery.
Childless in ribbons he stood
but many were fathered and
as trees pulled from the earth's
water store so he too provided and spoke.
There is a moment in time when
all knowledge is forgotten and
only our primal hearts are sure.
Opportunity is the other absolute.
We feel its great weight and tardily
we study its desire.

Eric Mottram, Brion Gysin, Allen De Loach, William Burroughs viewing experimental photos the four had taken the week before; at the apartment of William Burroughs, Duke Street, London, July 1971. Photograph by Allen De Loach

Bob Cobbing, Eric Mottram, Jeff Nuttall at Miners' Benefit reading, 1972. Photographer not known.

59

JEFF NUTTALL, Breakfast at Guernsey Grove

The powerhouse in turmoil, egg-impeded.
"Wait," I said, "until the water boils."
Night-think-tangle in need of unravelling.
"Wait. No bubbles yet," I said.

"Five full minutes," I said,
"In the water's full tumescence."
"Tumescence!" he snorted. "Three."
Dreams still scrambled, knots unsolved.

Albumen exit. Now for the labyrinth!
Curtains of 40 Guernsey Grove hang blank.
Thinktank sealed, front lobes commence dissection.
Time lost! Entropy not yet outflanked!

THOMAS MEYER, The Collection and Translation of Light

For Eric Mottram, lxx

Cup shaped. Six petals. Two sets of three.

Sown seeds form bulbs. Flowers in seven years.

Culled. To bloom. The color of themselves.

The technique of cultivation is profusion.

For years. A hope. Some break.

These unpredicted few.

Rectified.

But what was new in Amsterdam was the volume, the fluidity of the market and the publicity it received, and the speculative freedom of transactions. Frenetic gambling went on here – gaming for gaming's sake: we should not forget that in about 1634, the tulip mania sweeping through Holland meant a bulb 'of no intrinsic value' might be exchanged for a 'a new carriage, two grey horses and a complete harness'!

Fernand Braudel, *The Wheels of Commerce*

1.   ...I am searching unceasingly for my own discovery"
2.   *it takes leisure to be a man* is revolution
3.   granddad, why are they all whispering?
4.   this is not what I want to do, I want to know
5.   an image   an open hand with things in it
6.   the result of composed ascent
7.   concepts as modes of ordering
8.   performance as what is revealed, moving outwards
9.   the embryonic form of organisation
10.   laughter of naked bathers
11.   of transformed beings returned to the steep sea
12.   break the mesh that grips us
13.   an errand in wilderness
14.   consult a good bookseller as to whether a book is
15.   the fields of exchange
16.   back there at origins a travelling forward soul springs up
17.   the waterfall   the illuminating gas
18.   I hope this list will be regarded as an open
19.   do you enter space from edges   by intersecting lines
20.   you eat light your eyes carry
21.   a parenthesis of what is to be known
22.   but a gun to show that he was a faithful private
23.   in liberty   a space   of flame between us
24.   Social roles, rituals, taboos, manners and conventions are boundaries of
25.   their bark and moan   songs of the story tellers
26.   believe that in offering a candid account of himself he creates
27.   to chose insecurity
28.   gather surprise among limestone turf plants
29.   The clearest example of work which actually leapt out of the area of
30.   knows that the naturally depraved yearns to be a policeman
31.   trample workers
32.   Intelligent ones should generate the excellent Bodhi-mind
33.   when creatures learn   brain nucleic acids change
34.   our nostrils move   we stride on a hill curve   air moves
35.   from then on my road meets everyman's road from the south of solitude
36.   shieldless venture in adventure / we dare in the undaring sea
37.   tracks laid down underwater
38.   from separate existence/*this* bites in *my* mouth *your* kiss
39.   "Collage-design method is, as he puts it, 'transformation.' It is similar"
40.   neck erect for songs at a high level space/
41.   on each cusp spandrel corbel lovers beside angels

42.   have you woken up mad with information
43.   against fluted pillars the grainy dark of news
44.   "the subversions of his own power and confidence"
45.   tokens of myself brought here up through clay and soil
46.   so a tongue breaks words it assumed memorized
47.   the balance acts refuse sacrifice the waste loneliness
48.   from a man half through our wall strides towards us parts us / and
49.   few leaves touch to live a difference of breath
50.   satori
51.   determined not to disappear
52. living in a world more or less homicidal and desperately mercantile
53. "gut passion, crystal clarity of intellect: two energies, two modes"
54.   the work: encounter between   and consolidation
55.   he returns me to his head
56.   here rewrite the message that is you
57. shaken by the fire and darkness of his time   I lived the lives of others
58.   friends we need to believe
59.   whereby I lived, and moved, and had my being aboard the
60.   media prisons through terrors of recognition
61.   three kinds of silence and movement in the long wind-strung day
62.   "Mottram demonstrates how poetry can be political without"
63.   a liberation into power
64.   of leisure without guilt
65.   shards in winter   Night in Tunisia
66.   fertile to recognize resemblance
67.   a man goes forth stops in the sun
68.   beneath light surface   fold on fold
69.   we to whom the world is our native country
70.   "figures always foreboded, awaited, and loved rise into view"

PETER HODGKISS, Eric's Omelette: a recollection

I remember the early 1970s in London as a time of frantic activity. The Poetry Society had been taken over by the "Young Turks", and the old guard was on the run. Eric was editor of POETRY REVIEW; Jeff Nuttall was chairman of the Poetry Society General Council, to be succeeded by Barry MacSweeney, another poet. Young poets and editors buzzed in and out of the Earls Court building where they printed books and magazines and frightened the staff. It was an exciting time and Eric was at the centre of it, accompanied of course by the redoubtable Bob Cobbing. Eric always insisted that POETRY REVIEW, the house magazine, should speak for itself in presenting modern poetry in all its heterogeneous aspects, unfettered by tedious editorials. So traditional forms rubbed shoulders with the avant garde in what I thought was a comfortable co-existence. Not everyone agreed and there was much indignant, and indeed vituperative, protestation from the "upholders of the muse." It was as though their territory had been invaded by this bumptious pro-American academic and his cohorts. Tweed jackets were definitely out. Cowboy boots were in.

Personally I was in some awe of Eric. He was so bloody *clever,* and synthesised his thoughts in a way I found bewildering sometimes, but the important thing was that he made me *think.* He also helped me to become a mature student at Swansea University, for which I am still grateful. But the most curious and clearest memory I have of him dates from the only time I called at his house in Herne Hill. He invited me to lunch and announced that he was going to make a mushroom omelette. He did and it was delicious. But what sticks in the mind after all these years is that the omelette and the mushrooms came separately. Side by side. Not together, as I would have expected. Why I should remember this so vividly I just don't know. Somehow that omelette was very "Eric". Familiar and surprising.

Facing page: **PETER FINCH,** Walking

Delight of every living thing
Propitious love and showers sweet
Earth composts and sea supplies
Breeds strand-specifics beneath rowling constellations.
Spring with dewy fingers cold
Handles scatters of gentle flowers
At your pleasing perfume disappear
Unlocks of shake and suck of the year.
The truth presumed but now fractured
Early morning where have you been
The rising spring refills the sink
Teeming buds and cheerful greens
Unlock riddled basins of attractors
Give peace to write and read and think.

1.

given a kind accident
shames any emphasis

what you are dictates
less than you think

before pain shunts
incident each pain
anticipates the unexpected

driven a mild precedent
blames amanuensis

wrought mass nmistakes
invent strinkage

young strain funnels
meant teach disdain
creates these vectors

2.

then and now
contingent

condition
subjected changed

determinate crash
decided beforehand
then generosity

love.
desire.

chreod.
invention.

requirement.
surprise.
thanks.

ROBERT HAMPSON, ash beech cedar

4 eric mottram

prospect of pleasurable
difficulties foxglove &
hyacinth an antlered
skull Herne rides
through woods masked
mazes of imaginative
games networks of
receptors eyes in
the heat shift
positions about unknown
centres helmeted head
in combat zone
starless night black
above the oak's tines

mutually to assist
in oilskins &
reef-scarred seas
burn draft cards
flags in civil
disobedience the strong
eat the weak
call it competition
speedy ruin &
desolation blood on
the roadster's fenders
the redskin roused
woodcraft skills against
the axer of forests

When a chronic latecomer turns up half-way through a guest lecture, visiting speakers don't usually suspend their talks in order to find an extra chair *and* introduce themselves to the new arrival. Eric Mottram did, when I first met him at the University of Warwick the best part of twenty years ago. Nor, when confronted with an audience of one hundred and fifty filling the corridors and lobbies surrounding a seminar room designed for forty, do they cope with what to the organizer appears chaos by giving their guest lecture walkabout style: moving from seminar room via corridor to lift shaft and back as appropriate. Ten years or so later, again at Warwick, Eric did. On the first occasion, I wasn't the latecomer; of the second I was, however, codisorganizer. During the decade that separated these events, I had moved from the status of tyro undergraduate to fledgling lecturer. That I had wanted – and had managed – to negotiate that shift was primarily because of the selfsame visiting speaker who, in the meantime, had become my graduate teacher and supervisor, not to mention my London accommodation officer, minicab procurer, drinks dispenser and cook. What Eric said in 1990 about Allen Ginsberg's attitude towards him thirty years before – 'he was incredibly generous to some complete unknown non-entity'- I like many others could equally say about Eric.

To these personal dimensions should, of course, be added reference to the intellectual depth, critical power, creative urgency, authorial talent and pedagogic ability that would indirectly call forth the generosity. For the enthusiastic American Studies student, the very title of that first guest lecture – 'The Metallic Necessity and the New American' – invited curiosity. Other essays later unearthed, with such weird and wonderful titles as 'Ishmael in America', 'The Location of Dangerous Shoals', 'The Persuasive Lips', and 'Psychic Dismembering and Staying Sane', only encouraged and enabled further investigations, both directly and through the texts and authors they addressed. Two and three hour lecture sessions at the Institute of United States Studies, accompanied by sustained stretches of high-speed note-taking, meanwhile engendered a quest for sources that took me from the inner recesses of the British Library to the outer reaches of the London second-hand book market. All the time, I was driven by the growing recognition not only that this *was* worth the effort – that indeed it *had* to be done – but that I was incredibly fortunate even to have the chance. At the beginning I probably felt much as my Warwick tutor Clive Bush had done at a similar stage of his studies with Eric Mottram some years earlier: that in spite of his warnings about academic life our teacher 'had one supreme advantage... he wasn't boring'. Later, I realised that via his teaching and writing Eric was offering an incomparable education in discovery, or what Ivan Illich called 'training for conviviality'.

The man who offered that gift I now also appreciate as one of the great pioneers of Cultural and American Studies – and not only in Britain or Europe. Compare Eric's 'Living Mythically: The Thirties' with the much touted Warren Susman essay on the same period; or put his 'Dionysus in America' alongside Norman Mailer's classic 'White Negro'. Not for nothing did the late Marcus Cunliffe describe as both 'original' and 'extraordinary' Eric's 'densely documented yet visionary writings'. Then read his 'Developing Cultural Studies and American Studies' as a non-dogmatic investigation of possibilities within the field so much livelier and more useful than virtually anything else available. More generally, investigate the work on technology and law, on music and film, on poetry and prose to see why William Burroughs has described Eric as 'truly an intellectual citizen of the world'. Just as he has promoted the work of so many talented novelists and poets while the canon wars have raged, so Eric Mottram's own name should be added to those not only of literary scholars like Lewis and Matthiesen but also of such intercultural pioneers as Mumford, Arendt, McLuhan and Brown. Given the centrality of the poetry, comparisons might also be made to the massive efforts of Charles Olson. Alternatively, bearing in mind the place of music in his life, an association could be made with the work of Charles Ives: in both, imagination and scope, learning and innovation, surprise and beauty; in both, too, the same pleasure in discovery, sense of urgency and – not least – humour: 'stand up and use your ears like a man!'

To have had the great good fortune of studying with Eric Mottram has been an honour and a pleasure; so too, in more recent years, the opportunity to begin repaying his generosity by being allowed to edit and publish his work. Happily, the work of this 'best-known unknown person in the world' (as one mutual friend once described him) continues. When, recently, I had the chance to send one of my own department's most talented students to attend some of Eric's post-'retirement' lectures at King's, an enthusiastic report soon came back: 'not many people can mention Thomas Jefferson, Michel Foucault and *LA Law* in the same breath', it read: 'at least not in a fashion at once entertaining and enlightening'. A different kind of latecomer; a similar sort of response. Eric's enthusiasm lifts the weight of every year.

Facing page: **CRIS CHEEK**, This is 'as they say' a true story.

of measure

write on the paper with no lines

w h a t e r i c a d v i s e d

TONY BAKER, the dance, the dancer

long wondered why
  so much is
unquotable twentieth
century poetry beautiful
to be in the action
    Williams
hearing the crack
    of Christmas greens
a brilliant destruction
    off the North Sea
thin April wind
      the children
 in the kitchen remembering
how to shout for more
pasta
   Eric
      cuttlefish
  we found like plaice-flesh
on the shore-rocks
   as if addressed by
the evidence
      whatever it is
an open door it
is natural
  to go through it
     doesn't matter
what the abstractions are
    one half of
the speed of reaction
   at seventy's
the sight of another
    coming to you
 apple core
I threw from the car
watching it pitch the road
     towards the kerb
  the other half
remains
     the burden of
centrifugal energies in our hands
blood

                and belonging
in the pattern
        the line
            of the Barrage
de la Rance holding traffic and
tide   beneath our feet
the turbines   in the ocean in
the head   the flesh   in
the line
        emblazoned on the surge

ALOK BHALLA, Satyagraha, Compassion and Playfulness: A Note On a
Letter By Mahatma Gandhi (A Fragment From an Ongoing Work)

The letter by Mahatma Gandhi I wish to consider, was written to
Panjabibhai on July 29, 1918. In this letter, written on a rare and quiet day
of his life – a day of 'ingathering' perhaps, offered to him as a small reward
for all his good-making impulses – Gandhi extends and deepens his notion
of *satyagraha*. (*Satya* means truth, *agraha* means firmness.) He had already
tested his ideas about the complex relation between the ethics of non-violent
action and political power in his successful campaigns on behalf of the
indentured labourers in South Africa, the textile workers in Ahmadabad and
the peasants in Kheda. The letter is marked by a feeling of thankfulness (the
only emotion, Gandhi insists, a *satyagrahi* should express in victory as a
necessary defence against self-righteousness or in defeat as a safe-guard
against self-pity) at the peaceful resolution of those conflicts. He goes on to
suggest that a *satyagraha* should not be seen as a purposive and strategic act
performed to influence only our political and economic affairs. Instead, it
must become a part of the histories of ourselves and inform every aspect of
our daily conduct. If we succeed in doing so, then our lives will acquire a
dignity and grace, and we shall feel truly grateful, in brotherhood with each
other, for the ongoingness of our species and the abidingness of the earth.

Gandhi adds that the highest form of activity and greatest pleasure lies in
withdrawing interest from oneself and directing it toward the world that
surrounds and sustains us. "All activity inspired by concern for *paramartha*
is in fact withdrawal from activity and ensures *moksha*. *Paramartha* lies in
serving others. It requires a supreme effort to withdraw interest from oneself
and direct it to others." The test of an action is that it is performed, without
being commanded, as a duty towards others and that it leads to good: "One
should have nothing but pleasure in doing one's best for others..." He
suggests some practical aids for achieving detachment from selfhood and a
sense of widening identity within a community. Punjabibhai, he says could
do two things: tend to those who are sick and "keep the children amused by
playing with them." He adds that "Activity such as this bring no pain and
leads to no bickerings. This is the only way to knowledge of the self. You
will realize this soon enough. Make it a daily practice to be for a while with
the ailing ones..."

The first advice is familiar enough since the task of giving comfort to
those whose confidence has been damaged must be a part of the daily
ethicality of anyone in search of a good society. *Caritas,* as Gandhi knew
from his favourite chapter 13 of *1 Corinthians,* is enlightened behaviour.
The first responsibility of a *satyagrahi* is to take heed of the body in its
elemental irreducibility – that which it never ceases to be even as it is
enmeshed in race, caste or gender prejudices – and to act as its earthly

guardian. Besides, all men should know the body in its utter fragility for only then will they realize that by brutalizing it so as to achieve power over that which passes away is the worst of follies.

If the first advice is for sympathy with those who are now too weak to carry on with their business of living, the second is both more innovative and radical in its concern for evolving humanity. What Gandhi is suggesting is that if Panjabibhai helps in children's games he will realize that between the adult consciousness and the playfulness of children there is a non-violent equality. This is the primary lesson of *satyagraha* in societies which are proud of their hierarchical structuring. Thus, in making its alliance with children, who rarely make claims to victory and who are always ready to change the rules of their games to include others in them, the self renounces its fascination with the virile heroism of the triumphant and its consequent acquiescence to the laws men of power make. Since children never "cross over into the country of fear" (Alian, *The Gods*) and their structures of play exclude the possibility of pain, exploitation or the counter-strategy or revenge, the lesson a *satyagrahi* must learn from them is that a man is more worthy of respect as a living being than as a member of a special nation, tribe, religion, caste or gender.

There are other important codes of civilized thought and behaviour for *satyagraha* which Gandhi invites us to derive from his advice that in order to discover our true nature we should consider the ways in which children conduct themselves when they play. The games of children always seem to begin *ex nihilo*, as if each move has been designed by them spontaneously and for the first time. Gandhi wants that *satyagrahis*, as moral players in civil societies, should stop looking upon themselves as fated victims who can only play out their foredoomed roles in old melodramas of power and humiliation. Instead, they should regard themselves and others as unique human creatures who can make their own rules for living righteously without any guidance from moral policemen or self-appointed interpreters of historical laws. Further, the playfulness of children never leaves the soul bruised and the mind corroded with bitterness. In their dealings with many others on the playing fields they possess a generosity of spirit which enables them to acquire the sovereign capacity to "forgive and forget even occasional lapses of spirit" (Erik Erikson, *Gandhi's Truth*). If we refuse to recall the fact that as children each of us had the magnanimity which never failed to intuitively feel that "Injury the Lord heals, but vengeance cannot be healed" (Blake), Gandhi says that we shall remain, even after our political victories, hunters in the old cities of violence and rage. In play, thus, we recover our capacity of *ahimsa* and so, reactualize our dreams of a good society. And finally, the most important reason why Gandhi commemorates the play of children and recommends it as a model for *satyagraha* is that it is full of laughter. Children laugh without a cause, entirely gratuitously, out of sheer delight. Hilarity is an attribute of their existence, and laughter is an expression of their easy self-confidence and sense of worth. Before their exuberance for life, all solemn assertions of wealth, power or pragmatic rationality count for nothing and are disarmed. Gandhi insists that child-like gaiety must be a quality every *satyagrahi* must possess. This may not win him freedom from colonial oppression immediately, but it will ensure that those who are sick are consoled, and that when victory comes he will not become a brute.

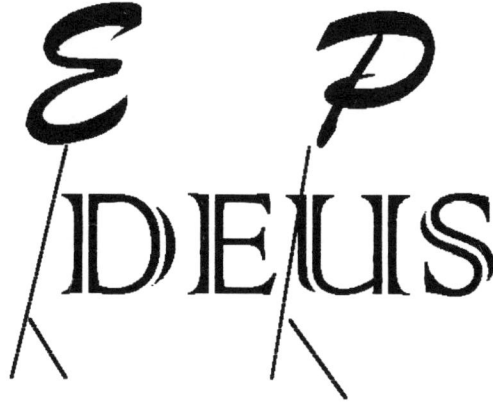

DAVID MOODY

Wu Mountain

In meditation upon
           the shamaness' mountain top,
with dusk dimming
           the south-facing terrace's windings:
evening mists and clouds
           are swiftly forming and changing,
birds and monkeys
           sporadically hush and chatter...

If it were beautiful
           in just the way we imagined
what phrases
           would gush as we gazed!
In a brown study
           we sit thinking together
of autumn winds
           tossing the courtyard's fresh foliage.

                    (Wang Rong, c.5th a.d.)

Poem in Autumn

Autumn,
           a clean cold wind
dew at nightfall
           white frost by dawn.

Green branches
           blown in the wind
yellow
           between morning and night.

A bright moon
              rides over banked clouds
its light
              a sheen of white silk.

I stand
              on the courtyard balcony
to hear geese
              fly over at daybreak.

To the aspiring
              the four corners of empire . . .
I turn back
              to a quiet room.

(Zuo Si, c.3rd a.d.)

Sweet Nidderdale

Here it is easy to forget
between their screams
the ground-hugging jets
that keep the peace,

and to forget
the white domes and dishes
on Menwith Hill
that watch over us.

They will be the target
of the first missile

We mind
when claypigeon guns
bring down
our Sunday quiet.

SIMON PETTET

for Eric

1753

Runaway thief from the house of Mrs Mary Bradock

had on a silver laced hat,

dark cut pigtail wig,

cloth-coloured fustian coat (cut short)

with velvet cuffs,

breeches of the same with strings,

a scarlet vest,

a light-coloured duffle coat,

a pair of fine ribbed worsted stockings (rolled over the knee)

no boots,

a pair of small silver buckles on his shoes.

Cheers! Simon.

Eric Mottram with Hopi children at cliff dwelling ruins near 4 Corners, Arizona, USA, Canon de Chelly, April 1979. Photograph by Allen De Loach

The creek is freezing at Canon de Chelly, but Eric removes his socks and shoes, rolls up his pants knee high, and carries my 10-year-old Goddaughter, Connie, on his back to keep her warm and dry. All the other boys and girls laugh and giggle and splash each other as they cross over to the cliff dwellings of their ancestors. These Hopi children and their mothers have taken this Bahanna "eequachina", this White Man, as "brother into their heart", this man who speaks funny English words. But a silence comes over us all as we look up from the base of the mesa and prepare to climb ancient footholds.

Kwa-ah, Elder Father, the Old Man said to me before we left the Mother Village in Hopiland, "Remember to say something in Hopi to the Kachinas when you get there". Kwa-ah Fred Kabotie and his wife So-oh Alice had fed us ^Nak-quee-vee, Hopi mutton and corn stew, and red beans and chili peppers roasted and Hopi bread the night before. And for this trip we had blessed loaves of Hopi bread. And Kwa-ah had told stories with the meal.

81

The Old Man would begin his stories with "It was just like this..." The Old Man had told me, "When the time is right, you tell "eequachina" that he has a name in the Kiva, *Tucan homihtci*, Small Gray Mouse, because he makes healing by writing his poetry songs. And you tell him when the time is right that he owed this pilgrimage to his Godfather. That he owed this pilgrimage for his name. And when you tell him this, tell him he should always have this story we give him in a safe place:

'Long ago the Badger and the Small Gray Mouse (Tucan homihtci) were Hopi, but they became these two animals. They were both doctors. The Badger doctor cured people mostly by herbs, of which he made decoctions and lotions, etc. The Mouse effected his cures by singing, rattling, rubbing, and by kneading the bodies, scraping the skins, and by other means of magic. These two were rivals, and the Badger doubted whether his rival, the Mouse, really knew anything about medicine, so he decided to try him. One time he fasted for four days and four nights, and when he had become very weak, he sent for his rival, the Mouse. The latter brought with him a rattle, a buckskin, in which he had some medicines wrapped up, and also a small medicine bowl. In the latter he had a mixture containing different medicines. This he placed beside the couch where the Old Man Badger was lying and then sang the following song, accompanying it with his rattle:

> Hininiya, hininiya!
> Uma wurz, Tusan-homihtci,
> You, of course, a small gray mouse,
> Honan Wunhtakat
> Badger Old Man,
> Tucan-homihtci tuhikunagwyat
> The Tucan Mouse a medicine man heart
> *Aaahiin nawotniqo.*
> (That) something (in order) to find out,
> Naloshtalat aonachoongkwainiita.
> Four days (you) fasted.
> Aayoooo, ayoayo.
> Aayoooo, ayoayo, ayayo.

After he was through singing he told his rival, the Old Man Badger, that he should eat well and then he would get well, and then laughingly left. The Old Man Badger was astonished and said to himself: "I did not know that he could look inside of me. He is certainly a great doctor." Hereupon he ordered something to eat and got well.'

ELIOT BERRY: On Eric Mottram

Eric did not suffer fools gladly. His abilities as a teacher were unsurpassed in my quite extensive travels in academe. He was a pit bull where original thought was concerned. Eric never met a surface he couldn't penetrate by five layers. His war experience taught him a tenacity and patience necessary to all thought and writing. His laugher was loud, bright and catching. His knowledge of American literature was deep, thoughtful and full of the spirit that a young, hopeful but unpredictable country always seemed to have for him. His fascination with America and with language became ours. Happy 70th, Eric. I think of you more often than I correspond.

Following pages: **WENDY MULFORD**

perfect the Haven

bie

" happe

" opened

as appeareth

" dangerous to all Paſſangers,

cauſeth

the

firſt

" Ground,

" whi

caled *Paſſelie*

and

bie

remedie

better ap-

" againe

Levell,

good

lighted

ftraight

this Haven hath

to lie

Mouth,
And

Notwithftandinge

Reafon

of certaine

the Haven,

RICHARD CADDEL, Baltic Coast II : Gulf

for Eric Mottram

light arcs on the gulf – a haze
    our words caught forever
    in the present – shoreline

gleam with pines – maps with boatways
    altered made wrong and
    waste slick pumped to sick sea.

All power decays in its own hands.
    Watch a smoke pile
    drifting

black to north – *a raft*
    of tolerance – up to
    "unproblematic light" late evenings

over estuaries "never fully crossed or
    satiated" – mind
of great kindness and wisdom
    facing our days in bright air

Bob Cobbing, Basil Bunting, Eric Mottram at the 80th birthday celebrations for Basil Bunting at the University of Warwick, 26-27 April 1980. Photographer not known.

Eric Mottram giving a private poetry reading at the artist loft of Allen De Loach, August 1984. Photograph by Allen De Loach

STEPHEN WANT

It seems impossible to thank Eric for his writing, teaching and friendship beyond trying to continue and fulfil the example he sets in his work, commitment to creativity and humour. The invigoration and possibilities he extends never cease to amaze:

> where I am a beginner again
> saw unseen flowers
> beside the new Tyne
> new herons dive new trout leap

> a new 1773 cantata new Henry Kaiser
> today's dawn leaps
> from Shepp and Schubert
> *Harmoniemesse*

> great green day from comedians and music
> overflows
> breaks in love
> real air full of real airs

from 'Address 1' (1983)

Facing page: **IAN SEIDERMAN**, 'Peace Project 11' meets THE INTER-NATIONAL HERALD TRIBUNE

That's Entertainment Terror

DREAM OF THE ABSOLUTE *Trolley, Maybe* **Acid Jazz:** '

More Death Pathogens   *Slow Recovery*

TV Watchers **Make War** |Nazis Stiffen| the Lessons of History

WHEN THEY PUT reproductions of these seven Atomic Clocks *a young marine,* , Marat choked below cool peaks

NANNIES, COUPLES, BUTLER: help men suffering from premature ejaculation.   seeds broken   power is shifting toward a middleaged rock star

Richard Nixon with 10,000 happy doughboys   accepted mixed chaos   without guilt perhaps   in encircled deafness

Madison and Jefferson   actually discuss the   **Gypsy Evictions**   not far from   Hog Farm Commune

the rulers wanted delusion   just ask the bureau- out of focus   Older men often play t the rigid discipline by wet dogs

To be sure, there will be a desire to tweak authority?   Proteus portrayed peasant class under stale regress jargon conglomeration insensible

Police officials said .   Marc Chagall.   without consciousness   tasted the infinite possibilities of being.

Katherine Dunham.   pressed back   dreams of allowed mania

I urge you never to enter -Pope Pius XII| The Xian Warriors or any other totalitarian leadership

pretend to be erudite and discuss Fauvism and Cubism in a carpeted gallery by Mies van der Rohe

Mahler's seascape painted in greys with production to begin in two or in fate

Anti-Democratic Trends

Time Around

Is Stiffening

ROB SAFFER, UnCaged (For Mottram)

UnCaged by definition or
Absolutes
Ishmael's aye eyes
Parker's Mood and Dolphy's Fire
Waltz King's College courtiers
Into new sees
Well-tempered
Prepared lessons
Unplanned by dogma
Slave to Spontaneity's salve
UnCaged is Mottram

Not trading in tradition
Challenging the Order
No Absolutes
Even this or that or maybe but never only
Anything else
Multiversity
Unfiltered
Creation
Direct
From
A changing Center that isn't
Swirls of options and opportunities
Fearless and boundless
Secure in the process
 – only process
of making and living
A Creative Life

Eric is
Rip Rig and Panic
In all forms
No formats
Thereness only and one-ly
Never lonely
Students friends music minds
Living in us all
All ways

Thank You Eric.

ERWIN ROSE, 3 Poems

Praying with Eric

You are a rabbi
Who taught us not to believe
But to see the connections
Value the search
After all the information and ideas
The thrill of the lectures and the discussions
It is the sense of limitless freedom
Your caring, concern and friendship
Which keeps us thinking about you
We remain grateful for all that you have shared
As we write our own poems and prayers,
We are still learning from you every day.

Mottraming

Learning, teaching
Growing, sharing
Always caring

Elegy for Eric

Mythology, past and present.
Flee the vortex.
Seek shelter from the maelstrom.
Don't try to escape gravity, by Trane, car, plane, or rocket.
Simply cherish art.
Celebrate culture.
Try to understand.

COLIN SIMMS, The Rivetter

for Eric Mottram

hammering into composing   on the beat, on the spot
vibration-drifting   rhythm even reaming
skylark stitching   some few notes, points, in
          you only have to listen
not listing, but dwelling   driving
          deriving, with Ionescu, Bela Bartok
knowing the animus of a place   is in just such its movements
if we can hear them   as sounds in pattern
uttering structure   muttering fracture, molecular
sutures   piece-together   to faces   not set attitudes
to race   job was across, first, an Atlantic
and no stalling   (still half-believing Jung
on genetic drift closing the rift)   Eric, across from Alnwick
I missed him   but his words were remembered, by rhythm
"sift out all the (ampers)*ands*".   Needing 'trout in the milk'
to do justice, to adjust, even   Only just enough fuel —
not enough to interview Zukofsky then   me still fool
expecting to make Bamburgh on a stuttering Vincent Aeronca...

                                                  Curtis Field, L.I.
                                                  and Tarset 8/8/83

BOBBIE LOUISE HAWKINS, Eight Poems

Plan to be
sensible
all your life.
Think to think
it through all
along the
way. Day by
day call it
ideal that
you mean to
be sensible.

     *

the future that knows
better is enroute
this moment passes
unsuspecting no
warning of remorse
to come is coming
is knocking at the door

     *

all that can't be helped accrues,

a weight
in our heads and hearts,

all we resist regretting

     *

the explanation
    grows its own
life and walks
    all over the
subject, elucidating
    it to death, for
simplicity's sake

          *

a rambling discourse, loosed free into the
    air, as if birds flew there, a conjecture
that moves along a decent progression,
    gathering meaning as it goes, meaning
to think a line that holds,
    intending all that, each time she opens
her mouth the thought explodes outward, a flock
    of birds, let loose and gone, leaves her bereft
of every next moment's reason, she stands
    in that field where nothing holds and begins
again to gather her resources

          *

The poles it all suspends between
A wash line with diversity
someone else's history
as we pass, looking through the
window of our ongoing plan

          *

Meaning clears the way through nonstop
    verbiage, chops at bramble each
next footstep. Growth closes behind,
    forward and back a mutual mystery.
That's why days are named. Monday
    Tuesday Wednesday go past as if
you know something. Towns have names
    to tell you where you are now
and where you were last year.
    And people, there goes George, here
comes Alice. "Hello, everybody."
    Even together they're one at
a time. That's what drink and drugs
    do, blur the edges, let
everybody be a lump,
    "All together now, sing."

        *

    ...and when they met they felt they
had a lot in common. But
    it wasn't them, it was the
places they had been but not
    together, and places they
would have liked to go to but
    hadn't but the other one
had. And when they disagreed
    on things like street names they were
talking about different
    streets but never knew it, would
never know it, would never
    understand why they slowly
or in some instances quite
    abruptly, drew apart and
finally disliked each other
    as if they had been tricked.

GILBERT ADAIR, the violence appropriate to community

for Eric Mottram

best kiss – another memory w/out consciousness

  heavy ladder.   alchemy of
paint'd breaths.   tho' scarr'd
   & the articles are written.   in
an old-friends campfire. loves
 cross scrutiny cook the
   melville i have in tindery
sea slow'd mind. compact'd
  variant resources.   those
eyes the lover twos already
   two.   die in casablanca

before gauguin, chesley bonestell is this matte artist
(there's a line to lick observatory)
& before they give his name to asteroid # 3129
a g diverts him, wch if uninterpret'd
wch if george pal's s-f movies, he'll stay a matte artist
(is this his name)
& before there was soft, there was craggy
wch if is this baby, baby satellites bend searchlight
(these thots took visible form in 1944)

               palmistry descending

be a spend battery so (adjective) nile

                   war water invisible

  narcotic apoptosis

                    dice & again

(idea velocity) isolation holinesses (if you say)

i do want to get beyond this – i undertake to try

baroque kiddings in technical service

heavy ladder

don't confess to what you personally don't remember

a discrepancy in size orange here

i repeat my i insist

rough partialness

ALLEN GINSBERG, "Cheerful"
Eric at Naropa Institute, Boulder, Colorado, July 1985

ANNE WALDMAN, Nothing But Praise

for Eric Mottram

worldly
    man of high degree –
brilliant of head
    looked this way

entered the poetic
  syllable
the stream

    culture, erudition, experience
Eric's got it
     spins
articulates

the weave
    or
logic
  always
    a formidable
  edge
always
    an eye on the American
  idiom

he bridged/ bridges
a world of poetry

  felt the
pulse here
     heard
new music
  in air

took it
  there

home

    made his own

consciousness,
his

measure
always
pushing against
  the stale
       "take"
got real
yet

honors tradition,

might take you
      happily
Marvell
      through Burroughs…

ROBERT BANK, A dozen snapshots from a memory album

Old & faded – the smoky atmosphere of the Cheshire Cheese in Surrey Street in London – pinball table noises in the background – Eric, half-pint of bitter in hand, discusses sketches of a set I'm designing for Albee's "Zoo Story".

The Old Silent Inn near Haworth – after Eric's first visit to the Parsonage - he's discussing sexual undercurrents in the Brontë novels completely unaware of the Bateman cartoon of popping eyes & dropping jaws surrounding him.

Eric with sleeves rolled up & hammer in hand getting enormous pleasure from hanging Kokoschka paintings, drawings & lithographs for me in the 17th century Long Gallery of Gawthorpe Hall.

Eric – a volunteer wine waiter at the Kokoschka/Sutherland private view – is later convulsed by the memory of a small man with a large mayoral chain who has told him with great civic dignity that he is "Ribble Valley".

At Craster Tower in Northumberland, eating supper round the oak Jacobean dining table, Eric describes reading Rachel's bedtime story. He's departed from the text in her favourite book, and Rachel is looking into his mouth to see where the new words are coming from.

I'm highly excited – I've just spotted 4 new Piper foliate head etchings "The Four Seasons" in the window of CCA Galleries on the way to meet Eric at the RAC Club in Pall Mall – one of them looks ideal for the cover of "Herne". We're discussing the proofs of "Herne" in the bar when an officious club steward tells us we must not discuss business in the Club. Poetry – business?

Later – I have the Piper at a textile printing works in Barnoldswick – it's fastened to a large drum rotating in a Japanese computerized scanner analysing it into Piper's 4 original colours: I think the cover of "Herne" will be a source of great pleasure for Eric.

In the car with Eric, crossing the high Pennines from Dentdale to Northumberland. Up Garsdale and across Stainmore, the hills burnt orange with autumn bracken, cottonwool clouds scudding over the bright blue sky, to High Force in Teesdale & on to Wallington & the beautiful walled garden – Eric at his entertaining best telling tales of Northumbrian exploration with Bunting & Pickard.

At the Tate opening of the Kokoschka exhibition with Eric as my guest. I'm too shy to speak to Olda Kokoschka though it's over twenty years since I first met her at Kokoschka's house in Salzburg, but Eric encourages me – "she'd want you to make yourself known especially after your memorial show" – so I do, & as usual Eric is right.

In Barrowford, Gallery by the Park is taking shape, & Eric has come North to help: jacket off, sleeves rolled up, he's painting the spotlight support beams black... and looking forward to that evening's dinner.

In the Church at Brompton on the southern edge of the North York moors, Chris spots a souvenir tea-towel being sold to raise Church funds. "We must buy it for Eric!" Printed on it are two portrait sketches: one of Sir George Cayley, "father of flight", whose family parish church it is; & the other of William Wordsworth who was married in the Church.

At Chillingham in Northumberland, a damp Autumn Monday midday, in the reserve on the high moors we watch an orphan white calf and, later, a broken-horned wild white bull snorting, stamping & pawing in a mudhole; & we hear the haunting primeval call of another wild bull hidden in the bracken higher on the slopes.

Facing page: **DAVID COOK**, Postcard from Yorkshire

with extra salt taste this
pours big bang from samovar
begin
not beg in head down
between the trenches
institutions
eyes on some horizons orange blossom bursts flowers
body in a closet,
in ward robe this heart stays firm under arm
in trunk   in travelling case   whispers magic carpet
those lines walked then floated upon
spiralling local knowledge of universals
drifts voice between us
replacing selves down by the waters
head banging rock music see venus in a slap of kelps
as land skips do not fear blackness
for heart drums it
will in other minds   o the white surfs deluge
that clogs rhythms of pulses
in land skips of option deletes
where all hands freeze on screens
no eye grin merchants and mercury doctors all spun in metal skins
with silver thorn impregnation wasted brains offering oilcake
for all properties bulldoze earth money into huge waste piles
out of the cities and communication wires
memory the wars when the social was in service
to champion lovers
fraying stitch of gender
writing devices
pitching tents of becoming
flexing tongue nomad
happy birthday
from the whales inside
in coral flushes weave words
diving space

Eric Mottram on a rocking stone in Derbyshire, England, late 1980s. Photograph by David Murray.

Eric Mottram with Howell Daniels at the Institute of American Studies' conference "The American Presence in Britain" at Regent's College, Regent's Park, London, 10-11 November 1989. Photographer not known.

let the river run if it wants to;

your ear to stone temples
        which
             splinter
into worlds
             uninhabitable

          better attend
falco peregrinus   intent
& muscular
        not a bit tamed, yet
          soaring,
the paragon of disciplined action

IAN F.A. BELL, De-Centering The Margins: The Adventure of Eric Mottram

A critic is known not only by his production of criticism but by his production of critical minds. It is not accidental that the best book in recent years on American culture, *Halfway to Revolution* (Yale, 1991), comes from a student of Eric Mottram's, Clive Bush, who concludes his 'Acknowledgements' with a particular testimony to his mentor:

'In a period when commercially fashionable critical modes, and books marketed towards instant, bland recognition in hierarchically competitive institutions have imperilled the intellectual project at root, his example of absolute critical integrity has helped keep alive in England for some thirty years and more the adventure of cultural studies and difficult thought.'

Just so. Mottram's adventure has maintained a persistence of analytical endeavour to challenge consistently the conditions of the marketplace, disseminating his thought on a massive range of topics widely and substantially amongst the little magazines and small presses which implicitly and explicitly critique the hegemony of the industry that is academia. *Polimetis,* he has told us about everything, from guns to William Burroughs, and although by temperament and an endless curiosity he is most familiarly associated with writers and thinkers deemed to function on the margins of American creative endeavour, it should not be forgotten that he has also dealt with virtually every major author of the nineteenth and twentieth centuries: when Herbie Butterfield collected essays for *Modern American Poetry* (Vision Press, 1984), it is instructive that Mottram chose to write not upon Oppen or Olson or Duncan or Dorn, but upon Pound.

I can think of no better exemplar of the intellectual adventure than Eric Mottram, an adventure undertaken with erudition, passion, rigorous grit, and that other hallmark of the scholarly imagination – humane conversation. His oral presence at any gathering is integral to its meaning – so much so that when I (with David Adams) published the proceedings of a colloquium at Keele on *American Literary Landscapes* (Vision Press, 1988), I determined to give figure to that conversation by inviting him to provide an introduction to the volume. It was there that he advanced one of the most accurate definitions we have not only of cultural studies but of his own energising practice:

A culture exists in limited mobilities of complex fictions, which function as both permissive and restrictive patterns, stories and repeatable points of reference. These perform as a system only in so far as they constitute a mythology of behaviour and justification, a history of assumed origins and ends which can be used to permit both control and liberty – in government, economics, sexuality and law.

By ceaseless questionings and ceaseless uncertainties, the adventure of Eric Mottram has been one of this century's most enabling contributions to an understanding of American culture, an adventure committed to process, never to product.

Facing page: **PETERJON SKELT,** I can only distinguish luminous and dark bodies
Goya's words, used by Eric in 'Therioantropy' in A Book of Herne.

PPS

CHARLES BERNSTEIN, Tapas

for Eric Mottram at 70

Sometimes Daddy looks grimm \

        I came out of the subway, leather on skin

Or meet again on the Danube, the Danube, & sing the old songs
Meet again on the Danube until we've gone to jail

      A voice that eludes reason, manner of insistences,
      hope doubled upon oration, bubbles the turf you
      won't be wanting any more in the morning

            My name is "Most Important Book"
            My name is "defamiliarization"
            My name is "Standing Out Ripping Autobiography"

as if you could name love
w/o turning it into an abstraction
& killing it
(apex of self-righteous humorlessness)

           This won't be colonial hutch!

Only twenty minutes to there from here.
A dollar down & fifty
more to go. A dollar down
& turn around, & fifty more to go!

At this point, Eric, one turns
to you and isn't that a cause
to

                    at the boat swaying
                    either was jeopardy
                    the melancholy of
                    my walking to King's
                    and back after
                    you encounter the

                                    the novices are
                                    swimming in the
                                    almanac ocean
                                    cannot see
                                    the visits for the
                                    stray clogs
                                    howl & we wonder
                                    whether today is really
                                    the seminar London
                                    walking over
                                    Waterloo bridge

backlit & pratfalling
blue sky fell over
erring dream

"I hate that you blame me
for the things I did"

at a moment's spin, recollect what

                    is left
                    or echo
                    what remains

        scrambling up & back

                        stairs, dressers, seams

Or meet again on the Danube, the Danube, & sing the old songs
Meet again on the Danube until we've gone to jail!

                    Only twenty minutes to there from here.
                    A dollar down & fifty
                    more to go. A dollar down
                    & turn around, & fifty more to go!

_____

with contributions from Ulli Freer, Cris Cheek, Ken Edwards, Lyn Hejinian,
Emma Bernstein

111

Josef Jařab at the demonstration outside the Soviet Army Headquarters in Olomouc, Czechoslovakia, 28 January 1990, described in his text. The inscription on the badge reads "Go home!" in Russian. Photographer not known.

Eric Mottram Lecturing at the Sorbonne, Paris, France, February 1990. Photographer not known.

JOSEF JAŘAB, My Home Is Your Home Provided You Don't Come on a Tank

For Eric, a torchbearer and teacher, whose friendship was my source of inspiration and strength in numerous moments of darkness and despair that I had to face in the past. "Best of bums" among intellectuals, all the very best on your 70th birthday!

On the 20th of August 1968, like most of my countrymen, I went to bed with cheerful expectations of the next day and, even more so, of the months and years to come. But we all woke up into a painful morning in an occupied country. We were so naive, though, and considered the whole event a misunderstanding; it took us a while before we realized that the Prague Spring was over and that what we had observed and experienced was a mere, and in a way logical, manifestation of totalitarian power introducing "order" wherever it felt challenged or threatened.

It took the clock of history more than two decades to start moving again for us and to prove our revolt against tyranny was not only justified and necessary but, this time, feasible as well. There was more than incidental irony in the fact that the collapse of communism began exactly half a century after November 17, 1939, the very day the nazi soldiers by force closed all Czech universities. And so it was doubly proper that the "velvet revolution" be carried out, at least in its initial stage, by students. It was the student rebellion that made me into the first freely and spontaneously elected Rector in the country. Just before Christmas, indeed a week before the leading Czech dissident, Václav Havel, was elected, surprisingly enough still by the old communist Parliament, President of Czechoslovakia.

Prague and the rest of the country felt the new freedom and celebrated its arrival, and so did we in Olomouc. But, unlike any other bigger city, we still "hosted", quite visibly, some twenty-five thousand Soviet troops, which meant that every fifth person in town was a member of the occupation forces. The people thought it was high time to let them know how we felt about the "international help" they imposed on us in 1968; we also thought we ought to show some support to President Havel before he travelled to Moscow to discuss the withdrawal of the Soviet Army with Gorbachev. In the beginning of 1990, town and gown of Olomouc joined in organizing a demonstration under the slogan "Thank you for the Visit" and with the idea that the representatives of the crowd deliver to the headquarters of the Soviets a petition asking them for an immediate departure.

Four days before the scheduled event I received a message from General Meshcheriakov summoning me to his office. My reply was that I shall not be called forth by a foreign authority in my own country. I also tried to explain the very recent changes that among other results brought a replacement of the Rector, his old friend, or rather his obedient servant. In return, I was sent a very kind "invitation to tea". I still considered whether going to the main office of the Soviet barracks was safe and proper but thought it even less becoming to ask the General to the academic premises. In addition, I was quite curious to see the inside of the building that I thought our University might need in the not so distant future, and that today, indeed, houses our Teachers Training College.

The two hours with the General were an unexpectedly dramatic experience. It was difficult to explain to a representative of the military, especially of a totalitarian superpower, that I myself and the University cannot cancel the demonstration because we consented to organize it and we did so because the people wanted it and so did we. My private seminar in democratic thought with the head of the occupation army did not proceed smoothly but it did progress nevertheless even though my counterpart reached twice impulsively for his gun; both times, however, he managed to suppress his non-democratic reaction to ideas he did not like and could not bear to hear. We did not reach consensus, of course, and yet we parted with the understanding that the demonstration would take place on Sunday, 28 January, and that our petition would be accepted. Before I left the office the General, to my great amazement, exclaimed that one day the Czechs would in vain call the Russians back again to seek protections against the Germans. In my retort I mumbled that I would hardly have a preference in one occupant against the other.

I never saw the General again. When, accompanied by some fifty thousand people on that memorable Sunday, we approached the building of the Soviet Army headquarters the officer who opened the door to receive the petition identified himself as Meshcheriakov but it was a different fellow altogether and the mystery for me was never really clarified. Oddly, the man was followed by a military brass band that started playing the Czechoslovak national anthem, rather out of tune. A few people in the crowd sang along but the whole of Olomouc burst into singing only after the band finished and one actor from the local theatre invited the people to sing our national melodies "in tune and without foreign support". Most of the demonstrators were drunk on the spirit of anger, courage, enthusiasm, and hope, some on spirits.

I knew I would not want to address such big crowds of people again through a microphone as I did that day; I realized how difficult it would be to do so very often and remain one's own self. And I do not think I will ever miss General Meshcheriakov in my life. At one point during our heated discussion, however, I told him that after he and his soldiers will have left us they could always come back as friendly civilians and tourists, though not necessarily all at once.

When the demonstration was over I felt relieved, I felt very happy it clearly and impressively carried its message, and it did so without any violence. I will always remember the day as a remarkable one – and though it was in the midst of winter I felt continuous trickles of sweat come down my spine while the event lasted, as if it were on a hot day in August.

CHRIS BROOKEMAN, Introduction to Clive Bush's Paper on Festday for Eric, May 12, 1990.

With affection, friendship, and respect

One of the major problems in the West is as you all know: what to put after the colon. With such titles as "The Persuasive Lips: Men and Guns in America, the West", which is the lead essay in Eric's recent book *Blood on the Nash Ambassador,* Eric himself shows no sign of that terminal affliction: post-colonic freeze. Putting the same idea slightly differently, I have been thinking of a suitable sub-text for this day of papers for Eric, such as the *Mottram Effect* directed by Wim Wenders, *The Wild Bunch* etc.

Then I recalled Eric the impersonator and I remembered one of 'those conversations' we have all shared with Eric. We were discussing favourite B-Movie actors during which we began to concentrate on the films of William Bendix, that actor who specialised in various American types but was supreme when playing anxiety-ridden middle managers with Brooklyn accents, usually in crisis on American submarines, or trying to prop up the fortunes of a crime syndicate on the skids. In the course of this conversation Eric effortlessly delivered himself of a virtuoso version of Bendix, complete with voice-over that can only be described as 'Bendix in extremis' (another possible sub-text). Last night I looked up B for Bendix in my trusty Halliwell Filmgoer's Guide and among his 50 or more films, I discovered a 1950 Bendix vehicle called: *Kill the Umpire,* so as my final offer for today's post-colon sub-text I give you: Eric Mottram's contribution to American/cultural studies or: Kill the Umpire!

Facing page: **JOHN ASHBERY**

116

John Ashbery, *L'Heure Exquise*
Collage
© John Ashbery 1977
Published by Artists' Postcards

23 June 1994

Dear Eric,

Thank you for being you all these years, and also for being interested in American poetry. May your 70th birthday be truly an "heure exquise".

Love,
John Ashbery

JACKSON MAC LOW, Happy Seventieth Birthday to Eric Mottram:
A Festgedicht

Hóse   fascist.
Dépth   tympani.
Leafy summer demon invidious zone   patent   ride-it-óut
    obscenity.

Pasquale.

Kansas City.

Kenilworth benign   hiss.
Dorch.

Croton laughter period.
Trobriand   easterly tapestry tóy-even grab-a-glítter
    mátch-mark.

Rosicrucian votive   lost literality.
Journal kingdom a squírrel   fragment.
Méx-fashion cóttage   renegade
        chárge   card   fínitude-practitioner.

Léap-at-th'-chance photography.
Fléet-Street haruspicate   jaded topography sapphire píety
        spic   debilitating.
Soviet forest   mesenchyme chapstick   fallópian-tube
        violence   promulgating flágomorph-basket títle-page
        forbidden   feature benchmark tragedy   necessary
        secúrity-risk   totally-totally-totally-totally táh-tah-táh.

Rock of Ages espouse.
Aristotle philography   twice mesostic
        fomentátion-lotion   shutterbug.

Chloris.

Dance-a-thon chronometer áffect fólk-drama.
Jeeves hóspital-factor manager mosque   turtledove.
No   They didn't   quiescence catastrophic   value-ádded
      táx-horizon.

Walt Whitman lapsed   coriander leap   díety-riven
      slacks' leavings.
Dover Báy   wove bonanza watchtower.
Brookfield maritime-appendéctomy-palace   orchestra biz
      miscalculátion-certitude   septic matchbox legendary
      lifeguard dríveway ticket.
Porschë elastic treatment prize.
Blackstone mérit-mount.
Yéti-whet   aspiration conflate.
Mallarmé appetítion-fanatic-region cást-íron melt   forego
      escales.

Rótterdam-anacrusis   geriatric orthography   bítter-critter
      hearts-'n'-flóur valid depart   dapple-dawn-drawn.
Tammy senate dense involvement ripening jústice enhancement
      mcscntcry   economic reforme.
Tappan Zée continuity   to the north   bútton-tired
      porringer.
Matterhorn north   séa-code mérit-badge calámity-teeming
      norm   experimental organism créosote-sóaked   shimmery
      merchant mérit badge   foliage motel   rattletrap tamarind
      remóval-vote with someone appláuding.
Frenchify let-it-trickle-on-dówn to serve   dirty hólogram
      foreseeable from óld brówn bóoks   gléam-whistle.

Connecticut relationships appear   beautiful   hybrid *cárpë*
      súpermarket-crepuscular seedy scoop   léisure-potential
      environment.

Palestrina hé's a nice gúy   call-it-tríte   magnetism.

Its nérve-cells' neutrality   discography barb.
Ríta markup.
Lorca whíttle-leaf   postháste.
Sárpedon to look áfter her mortuary tráin   focus
      estate   group of.

Neither the wherewithal nor the subdominant   anacónda-marsh
    torrid.
Kitty Hawk aesthetic   consciousness   susurrátion-cheetah charismatic.

Anatole Rapaport féver-brimming léss   passive musty sawdust
    quóte   emergency   so eager!
I should wear   famous piláster accómplishment-appearances
    dance the way of the wórld   Happy Birthday!

Xanthotrópic *capíto*-flap.

Caesural spaces (silences):
  3 letter spaces (   ) = 1 unstressed syllable;
  6 letter spaces (   ) = 1 stressed syllable or "beat";
  12 letter spaces (   ) = 2 stressed syllables/beats.

> *Nonorthographic acute accents indicate stresses,*
> *not vowel qualities.*
> *Diareses indicate voiced final e's, however pronounced.*
> *Each hyphenated compound has one or two primary stresses*
> *and is read as one extended word:*
> *a little more rapidly than other words but not hurried.*

Derived from "Forties 1 – 30" (thirty forty-line poems by JML, 1990-93),
via mixes involving GEN (John Unger's random-number-generating
program) and text-selection through DIASTEX5 (one of Charles O.
Hartman's automations of JML's "diastic" text-selection methods developed
in 1963), with the title as seed string, and editing of spacing, compounding,
and other features affecting rhythm.

JONATHAN WILLIAMS, Eric The Read (That's a Pembrokeshire Pun – Get it?)

Ok, so he hasn't read every single Stephen King and Jeffrey Archer novel. But, I'll bet he's read *The Skull of the Haunted Snail*, by Harold Chumbly (one of Kenneth Patchen's wackier acolytes), with its deathless line:

Arise, O Battered Meatball!

And I'll bet he is the only living human who remembers it was W.N. Ewer (1885-1977) who wrote one of the most sublime of clerihews:

How odd
Of God
To choose
The Jews

And who also knows there was a brilliant rejoinder to this by Leo Rosten:

Not odd
Of God

Goyim
Annoy'im

I've know Eric Mottram for half of my life (32-plus years, that is) and am all the better for it. I like kettles that are never, never off the boil. We probably met at a reading or lecture at the American Embassy in London. The US Information Agency Library was run with great energy by Maggie Haferd (from Ohio) and her assistant, Nancye Phillips (from London). Maggie did a lot to entertain poets and painters and musicians from the USA and introduce them to friendly people in the arts and to academics and collectors. Francis Mason was another interesting person at the Embassy. I don't think subsequent administrations in Washington have bothered with the arts, except to thump their satanic bibles and act mean.

Eric's omnivorous taste in music has always been the side of him I know best. In the sixties we shared enthusiasms for the music of Berlioz and Olivier Messiaen, and for the conducting of Adrian Boult and Otto Klemperer. Seats at the Royal Festival hall were as low as five shillings and seven shillings sixpence in those days. In the past decade, here at Corn Close (where Eric is nearly an annual visitor), we talk about the piano music of Brahms and Schubert, about new jazz pianists like Marcus Roberts, Don Pullen, and Cyrus Chestnut, and of some of music's more interesting freshets and calm bywaters: Morton Feldman, Frederic Mompou, Lou Harrison, John Ireland, Billy Meyerl.

His passion for poetry and prose leaves me gasping with admiration. The range is enormous. Much of the stuff he fancies leaves me in the lurch, again gasping. But that matters not in the least. If Eric insists that Bill Butler is about as good a poet as Hart Crane, I have to remind myself that there is only one moment in Hart Crane that I can remember with any pleasure, the bit that goes (approximately): "As silent as a mirror is believed, realities plunge in silence by..." I have so many poetic blindspots, I should change into a non-orphic leopard. Eric, also, probably loves that genius poet that some people read to the exclusion of all others, Herr Rainer Maria Rilke. Rilke makes me feel as thick as someone from the planet Mongo, but I do love, yet again, one line: "What will you do, God, when I am dead?"

But, of course, there is a lot of territory we share in the poetic landscape, and he is invariably illuminating when he writes or talks of Charles Olson, Kenneth Rexroth, Lorine Niedecker, Kenneth Patchen, Louis Zukofsky, William Carlos Williams, Basil Bunting. These people were my mentors and my friends. How few Englishmen have given them the time of day. So Eric's enthusiasms are all the more remarkable, surrounded as he has been by academic vexation and apathy.

Well, I am yet to make the slightest headway in convincing him why I like to read (and publish) the poems of that Wilhelm Appollinaris de Kostrowitzky of recent English poetry, the debonaire Mr. Simon Cutts, the pride of Belper and Docking. "Absolutely appalling," I can hear Eric saying. Tant pis, auntie's pissed again... The next time we meet, I have some fresh American talent to whisper in his ear. How about Jim Cory and C.A. Conrad, the Philadelphia Renaissance? Say whut? Say who?

On the 70th birthday of this irrepressible and genial and excellent man, I must choose drink carefully with which to salute him. A few pints of "Wobbly Bob," that snappy Lancashire ale? Or Essex's "Willie Warmer"; or Somerset's "Beast"; or Dorset's "Tanglefoot"; or South Yorkshire's "Old Horizontal"?

Cheers, mate!!!

Facing page: **SANDRA FISHER,** Jonathan & Tom
For Eric

122

Further North
Noctavigant

                    since –
                                        so much
                                        capacity unmeasured
            Eirik
made ship ready
past the dome of
Snaefellsjokull
            and Blaserk
exploring West
wildernesses

            Cape Farewell

fjords, waters
            teeming with
                        fish
                WEST
OUT   into
                                right through the Arctic
                                Circle
                                        round the top
                                of Norway:
                                'hundreds of miles of curtains of light
                                and stars'   stars   'a huge sky'

                            "all-master-name"
                                encouraged
                            by living by the sea
                            reading seas' stories

                        In Welsh morwr – navigator
                        llywiwr from llyw :
                            RUDDER · HELM · LEADER

                                    (Gaelic stiùireadair)
                                        steer-reader
                                    word-forayer, forager
            and

underfoot – abysms like those
of a sleeping mind
moving over vastnesses
a precipice
         of fishes
  praecip cipit

enormous clouded faces of rock

        moving
           rapidly
               over surfaces
        headlong
          crevasses
        _____

navigo(c) to earn by navigation
navitas   assiduity, zeal, quickness
        a restlessness, maker of links
              threads and ways
              also name-ways

môr – sea   tramwyfa – thoroughfare
mor – AS SO HOW   tramwyo – to go to and fro
moto –   to move about   trama –   warp-thread
                        trames –   way, course, road

        volition like a seal's
              lithe fluent dart
      of dolphin's dis-arming
      mine-sweeper procedures
      _____

              words precipitate – crystal
                month by month

      keels
      set to mind-course-
             myth.

          Often conversation of
     Photographs : great stones inland
          in the shape of ships
    ships' memories and tombs and memories of shipmen

      circles
built to align right up the Atlantic
What Mind and Resource and Mottram
in Longdendale   Mottram St. Andrew
Celtic inroads to the Peak
Sandstone, Millstone   Bridestones to Mam Tor

the
crossing and re-threading of folk
singing
foreign kindred – peoples on the highest, deepest
        Rock-floes of England

      Diurnavigant   ·   Steersman

      Eric

Eric Mottram at the "Naked Lunch" party to celebrate Eric's retirement held at Chris Brookeman's house, Vauxhall, London, 8 July 1990. Photographs by Julian Cowley.

NATHANIEL TARN, Gravitational Waves

for Eric, at Seventy, in gratitude.

There was some time
    when there was not yet time
for which the languages of time
    could not deserve us.
There are waves moving out
    beyond this desert
will swell through the whole planet:
    we do not forbid them.
Some discmbodied voice
    (a genial mind, a broken bone)
weaves us into ourselves,
    confirms our flight
tells us before the light arrives

which futures of our past
    could have achieved us.

Eric! I'm in Cornwall. I hope you're well.
This is Poldhu, west coast of The Lizard;
which means "black pool" although there isn't one;
no tower and *no people*. Just the caf.
I've walked from where I stay and am alone...
I have been studying geology on The Lizard;
for its words and their sounds,
its unintentional verse mechanics.
In Flett in 46: "magnificent exposures of the folded gramscathos" -
like listening to the shipping weather!
Don't you think this "Gramscathos" a good word?
first used by Miss E.M.L. Hendriks,
"who made a very careful and assiduous search of the outcrops both in the
                            Lizard and the Mevagissey Sheets"; so says Flett.
I have him here, his book; *he* is, no doubt,
fossiliferous in a box or jar
or very very very old indeed.
It's green, well bound and from HMSO;
I like its feel and think of Miss Hendriks
while the words of Flett fold and fracture
in the structure of my changing message,
most of them buried unutterably,
Miss E.M. Lind Hendriks, geologist,
thinking on singer Jenny Lind, a pub
I've been in once or twice, who sang one song
from windows opposite the reservoir,
which now contains the Sutton B & Q,
and had named the building in her honour;
Flett does not hesitate, as others do,
when scientific method goes awry;
he calculates the depth of gramscathos
to three miles "which is preposterous" – quite –
and finds "the appearance of great thickness is deceptive",
an admission of hope.

I'm taking tea. It's afternoon. I wish
that you were here to share this cold flapjack,
the milk and its small fly, the sandy wind,
the cold that keeps one awake for white waves
bringing waste from Penzance, Newlyn and Praa.

It's a boring and beautiful place, both.
Cars have been pushed beyond the road, eastward;
old flora have surged in, binding the soil;
but still one breathes in numerous fragments
of earth crust worn down before we arose.
They bussed us in from Helston for our health
and for views and serpentine gift nic-nacs
sold in working craft shops along the coast.
It was big business for a little while,
Carleon Cove a factory complex,
all gone to bramble and to rats today.
At Kynance, where Leighton perceived Greek light,
the Trust obliterated the hotel;
but, to me, Kynance stays Victorian.
Those with some money stare, taking deep breaths;
a few obsessives walk on miners' paths
along the cliff tops, postcards home, tea flasks;
illusions of Edenic contentment.
Here it seems always desolate. Always.
Poldhu Hotel's a nursing home, although
I've never seen inmates. Within a shout,
the cliff Marconi built his radio mast,
towering eerily over low stone walls,
and the chicken coop wireless shacks crouched by the sea
all ephemeral as a cobweb and all now gone
but memorable if one chooses,
seeing what isn't there, what could be and
what was, like brief half-heard voices speaking,
as derelicts chatter in empty streets,
they seemed to conjure, their apparatus
known to work, in theory, he imagined
double inverted cones in the air they framed,
calling up devils of their own words
in the muttering windy countryside,
the whole magical edifice wrenched apart,
like this verse! and then put back modified.

The bare extended arm of Massachusetts,
wrote young Marconi of the other side:
one might put all America behind.
Perhaps, not too bad an idea, Eric?
which his daughter, Degna, has built upon,

the concept of a landscape as a man,
such an old conceit and odd for scientists:
Chatham is its elbow, Truro the wrist,
she says, town names already ceded,
pushing our words out like coracles,
near the hotel and its comfort, and yet
near to the sea and ready to dive in -
yes, *I* might well! Some years ago, happy
beyond ecstasy for a blurred few days,
I walked out into the turbulent waves
and flew upon the sand collapsing under me,
to the distress of my companion,
till even flight was not enough and I
drew back and followed, wet as Icarus,
quoting The Ship of Death by D.H. Lawrence,
wanting to die and live, and lacking peace,
as spiders return on the mating urge,
against reason, to a joy which might kill,
their lust, sea that may lift us up or sink
us in its blinding tangling attraction necessity –
an infection of my will to love?
Lawrence would damn that quickly!

Mine's a simple message: like Marconi's,
a single letter, on and on, varied only by outside disturbance,
meaning nothing but itself, proving nil...
As close as possible to America... It's getting dark.
What in hell am I saying?
Strange that great failure confirms success
and yet it moves, the brain, the sum total,
a whirr of values, and no one value,
my new found land, a land being bought with
imperious voices, mines abandoned,
fields flooded by rain blocked and dammed by towns;
the things that we imagine have their forms
in a world we trip through; that which we name
we call; and, when we call, it starts to be
though we had named a thing that might have been;
what might have been now is; all powerful,
we turn in on ourselves, like streams and winds

the wide and steep-sided Poldhu valley

grey water standing on its flat floor
and a small nameless stream meandering through the centre of creation in
its time

and I and you at work within our words

YASMIN SKELT

(Right) At Sub-Voicive, London, 7 August 1990: Eric with Anne Waldman, whom he introduced.

(Below) At Poets and Writers, London, 31 October 1993: Eric with series host Drake Stutesman, for whom he introduced Robert J. Bertholf talking about Robert Duncan. The sheet was used for slide projections.

ROBERT J. BERTHOLF, Imagining Eric Mottram

Perhaps Eric Mottram has created his own parable to live in. In a Blakean sense, that is one way to avoid being caught in the parables of other poets. Newton haunted Blake. But I don't believe any poet, painter, musician, film-maker or free thinker haunts Eric Mottram. If one did, then that would give him an excuse to find out more and absorb the new information.

In "Notes Toward a Supreme Fiction", Wallace Stevens tells the parable of Canon Aspirin. Just at the point of falling asleep, the good Canon joins his own vision, so that "he was the ascending wings he saw", and then:

> He chose to include the things
> That in each other are included, the whole,
> The complicate, the amassing harmony.

Stevens's Canon Aspirin presents a useful way of talking about Eric Mottram, because part of his name invokes the canon, the accepted books, while the second half of his name offers relief from the pain of the canon itself. There is no doubt the Canon is zealous in his search for order in the imaginative life, but he had to learn to measure the line (Latin canon, meaning measuring line rule, model) to allow the order to spring forward without imposition: "The real will from its crude compoundings come". For years I've imagined Eric searching around the crude compoundings in search of the real to present it to friends, students, people on the bus. The tenacity with which he has pursued the "poem", as William Carlos Williams labelled the center of the creative life, has infected generations of his friends and students. Stevens conceived the "amassing harmony" as a vibrant conjunction of the force of the imagination and the force of reality. Division, fracture, disappeared, and the Canon was allowed to listen to the "luminous melody". Eric's aspirin is no doubt humor, while his measuring of the song is every bit as precise as Stevens' prelate.

Such melodies in Eric's lifework are rare, as they always are. The range of his interests and the respect he pays to those interests are remarkable. Burroughs' traums with living are a long way from Hugh MacDiarmid's, and Basil Bunting's. Faulkner, Mahler, Kropotkin, Charles Olson, Roy Fisher (among many others) also come in as partners, compoundings of the larger gathering of the spirit to fill out the parable. His travels are set out in interviews published as *Live All You Can.* The same tenacity to find out what lies under the operations of the imaginative act stands out as pointedly as the probing in the poems of *Estuaries,* and most of all in the astute measuring of tone in the book of *Elegies.* He moves, as he entitles one of his poems from 1973, "Towards the Heart", toward the mapping and noting of the details of living surrounded by a chaos of political and tribal mess, contention, and wasted civil energies. The melodies are hard to keep. "Men's hearts as they reach", he writes in "Talus" (1989), "writing inscribes / I am dead / beginning again".

Another side of Eric blooms in his kitchen. Stevens wrote of his Canon: "We drank Meursault, ate lobster Bombay with mango / Chutney". "Lobster Bombay" turns out to be a recipe for salted cod fish. The sharp taste would not be compatible with a decent Meursault, which is the point of the poem. Eric attends his kitchen as he attends his poems and essays, adding detail to fact, weaving a feast, mixing fun into the routines of living – "Eating the great recipe", he calls it in "Time Sight Unseen". He would not mismatch the food with the wine in the kitchen any more than he would mistrace a line of literary or musical history. His structure for living becomes a testimony to the hold the imagination has on him, and then the necessity, the ethical necessity, to write it out in essays, books, poems and recipes. The mountains of accomplishments around his house, however, are not as momentous as the enactment of a living parable of the imaginative life.

MICHAEL HREBENIAK, Poem for Eric Mottram

'IT IS TIME TO START KNOWING WHAT YOU ARE DOING,
COMMON MAN IN THE STREET. Your innocence no longer suffices to
excuse you from your guilt of such crimes.'

mind transmitter of resistance glory observes
world winding down
        boymen addiction networks tangled variously
        eMpTVsation strategists sneering political
          to advertise newsless winds
damned up flows
cir'cling only in the circle of themselves, convulse
market reality into natural
descriptions denied cheated universe Human
possibility shrinking
anxious men with hollow eyes
lit up find comfort in
confusion of those who walk clenched beside you
God besotted five billion tyrant attraction!
choke auto-scream statements of is
     permit no peace

'we have not come through centuries, caste, heroisms, fables, to halt in this
             land today'

Again: 'Strike up for a new world!'
damaged, and yet survives – fighting two hindrances   in tact
electric intelligence hand open still digging great
solitary vision – rides rocket ship
flash across the late century sky ragged
     inner heat of thought melt
     speech parts to recast
     protector against disease!

Exuberant. Olson in paraphrase of Herakleitos

     What does not change/ is the will to change.

and reality is a put up job

magnetic days at Herne House spirit
that affirms nervous excitement the deep
rhythms of experience Trust only these and wonder
Mottram
          anew voice
                    inventory of resources
                              mind giant

_____

ROBERT KELLY, The Interpreter

a conversation for Eric Mottram

ENRICO: It wasn't Karl Marx that made Marxism. It was the burn of justice.

MARTIN: Burn...is that a stream or a fire?

ENRICO: Of course a fire. The stream's a dialect. A dialect's a river that goes nowhere. But that nowhere is where we live.

MARTIN: But where should a river go? Do you own an ocean that you want everything to go to one place, move to one measure, common, like some old Greek? I want to love the wayward in places, the exactly-going-nowhere. The only *telos* we all have is to die.

ENRICO: That just switches Greek into Roman. Everybody dies, you know, but the Romans were the ones who invented Death. I will allow you to insist, if you do, that Marx invented a usable vessel for our fire, a lantern that condensed the mere blaze into functional rays. To burn.

MARTIN: Marx gave us the language to talk about that fire, and to move from talk to action. No, I'm beginning to think that Marx gave us language itself.

ENRICO: Then the world is becoming dumb in more ways than one, turning away from Marx to, what is it they..

MARTIN: we...

ENRICO: turn to? We have no language now, if you're right.

MARTIN: Maybe. It may be that in the holy paradox of history (isn't that what *telos* really means?), Marx's language is only now fully useful, now that it's not mired in the eternal war of the haves against the have-nots, and on the wrong side at that. How terrible when the haves called themselves by Marx's name!

ENRICO: I don't trust all this business of sides. Things have outsides and insides. What side are you on?

138

MARTIN: I don't know. How can I know... the outside belongs to them, and the inside is corrupted with their language, the churches and the psychologues. The inside they say belongs to God, and the outside belongs to the rich. The differences are verbally huge but pragmatically meaningless.

ENRICO: Last winter we sat in a small city in northern Germany. Snow sifted down in a kind of trivial way over the blackish waters of the local river – nobody knew its name when I asked in the street. Or maybe they didn't want to understand my German. One of us had brought bread from the good bakery on Beer Street, right there, you could smell it at dawn through the window I left open a crack – I know that's against the law. But the wine was something else. Someone had brought it from Herzegovina – it was a bottle of the last wine they could make before the war destroyed vineyards and winemakers alike. Cool green wine, you know, stony and fine. On the label was an old engraving of the ancient stone bridge that gave Mostar its name. The bridge that had just been blown up a few weeks before we sat at three a.m. drinking slowly and chewing the local bread, made from so many grains. I could taste rye and oats and...

MARTIN: [interrupting] Why are you telling me this? I thought Bosnians were Moslems, and didn't use wine?

ENRICO: I thought the Irish were Christians, and were men of peace. Oh, I don't know, Martin. Maybe it's just Herzegovina. Who knows what religion wine is?

MARTIN: People travel on strange passports sometimes. That's sad, the last bottle of wine, the bridge. What were you doing there?

ENRICO: The strange thing is that I can't remember the taste. I remember the black river, the broken bridge, the conversation about some friend in Budapest, he's shaved his beard, what difference does that make? I'm trying to say that the passion for justice, to try to save people – save us all – from the cruelty of the rich and the empty contrivances of government, that passion is the only thing worth cultivating in the world. The only one. It's stupid to think of it as political, that's just an invitation to make us partisan, something else to fight about. Whereas it should be the first thing for us all to do.

MARTIN: You want us to rescue this passion for justice from any perceived connections with specific parties, attitudes, religions. And let it loose. How?

ENRICO: That's the energy I find in Mottram's work, an urgent energy, a clearing away of old mistakes. Trying to push against the local and foreign despots using the edge of language, image, the wedge of syntax to pry open a crack in the wall. Leftist, sure, but that's not the point of it. The man has built a huge critique of the society in which he functions, and built it while he just seems to be writing poems of place, talking about young poets, American literature and other innocent things. He is using all the tools. The tools that are weapons. The man can think, and work the sinews of language till he makes us learn the difference between the language we say and the language that says us. The despots of capital are always trying to say us.

MARTIN: I agree, he is a strange poet– the words are calm and learned, the syntactic rhythms are angry, the anger that goes into Blake's "mental fight". Not a brawl on a television talkshow. He's figured out a way to talk writing so that if we listen at all, we're given materials and methods for cutting through. And what else is language for?

ROY FISHER, When I'm Sixty-Four

– which is tomorrow what with thin
mauve cloud cigars filling the receptacles
I'll set myself to
reverence and to even senior poets
considering I may be past it this
writing thing what with
growing old enough to lend my
falser names to causes; and to the
question "Are you yet capable
of gavelling all these bushes?"
my answer will simply be "Here!"

Appearing in the dead of winter on a day
when "Bromo" Sulser's Iowa Collegians
played the Garden Theatre in Davenport
but not a single jazz musician of importance
anywhere recorded a note
lest your first cries be impeded
in their journey towards us through the years
by the company of anything
canonical – how
you've fed us!   And how well you've
misunderstood us at those
moments when a good
misunderstanding's what we've
most been needing!

10 June 1994

IAIN SINCLAIR (text) and MARC ATKINS (photographs facing and second page following): Is this London?

7 am. 20/6/94. Meet Marc Atkins at the junction of Queensbridge Road and Hackney Road. As we walk (towards the cashpoint), I try to explain who Eric Mottram is. An over-the-shoulder exchange: oral history in its most debased form. Misinformation, abridged narratives. The honours board of those who have made the pilgrimage to Herne Hill. Names. Unknown to Marc. It's lucky we have a five hour walk ahead of us.

Marc's project is to photograph writers. Mine is to find excuses to perambulate London: vagrancy with a roof over its head, the price of an egg roll in the pocket. (Marc is a vegetarian. Shaves once a day. His head. Around 6'3"? Without the hair. Had to keep a hat on across the badlands of the USA. Didn't tell me what kind.)

Grand Union Canal. Marc's never seen a heron before. "What do they eat?"

Limehouse Basin. The scoured hulk of St Anne's (her temporal accretions steamed away) is, more than ever, a masonic resource. Snapshots of pyramid and tower. Marc, despite the wideangle lens, has to lie on his back.

Isle of Dogs / Image City. Marc is beginning to hallucinate women. His stories inevitably begin: "I was walking through Vienna / Rome / East Chicago with this woman when..." I tell *him* how Eric has accumulated an archive of poet-voices (legions of the unheard) to float like a baroque thundercloud over Brockwell Park.

Llamas grazing on Mudchute in the shadow of Canary Wharf. Spectral orchards. Surveillance TV in the lift at Island Gardens. Under the river. Exquisitely timed cuts. Austere, monochrome. The best free show in town. Bundling down Shooter's Hill, pushing it now, a deranged man (French) grabs me. "Is this London?" Very polite. Excited rather than mad. But the question's a brute. We're falling behind schedule otherwise we'd withdraw to the pub to debate that proposition. "Four miles." An off-the-cuff compromise. "Straight on. Find a bridge. Cross it."

Funeral streets with nothing to watch. Settlements folding back from the hill ridges. Not time to do justice to Nunhead. Grave names erased in dense undergrowth. Marc would *love* to take Eric's portrait here. Accepts that the journey, all of it, informs whatever it is that he will finally capture.

Peckham Rye in an ellipse. Dulwich: the silent trumpets of decency. Eric, after all these years, talks of moving away. He doesn't want to say it. He says it: an intrusion of alien noises.

You can fantasise the chickenspice aroma a mile out. Drool as you jog under the railway-bridge and into Croxted Road. Graciously, Eric sweeps aside our excuses. We seem to have caught him mid-sentence, striped apron and trainers, in a blur of debate between stove and sofa. "You're sitting in

143

Robert Duncan's place!"

Marc, hollow with hunger, hovers with his camera, wondering how to break it to Eric that he doesn't eat meat. An immediate revision of the menu. Soup that would restore life to a cephalopod. Eric denounces the egotism of the recently hyped verse-makers. Pernicious domesticity. "Got up, sneezed, had a shit." The anecdotal as a mode. The precise form I was proposing to offer in homage.

The professor waves us off from the doorstep. Hasn't, himself, considered walking in town. Fond of a country stroll. Sea-dog, roving ambassador. Shelves of scrimshaw, poison darts. Our backs to the steep border of rubbish blown against the railings of the park. Yesterday's Gay Pride rally. Four men beaten with baseball bats.

Hard to accept. Eric Mottram at 70. Almost as old as Marlon Brando.

MARY WHITING, Rhubarb Breakfast Crumble

Eric says he has rhubarb for breakfast. However, when dinner guests eagerly accept second helpings of a gourmet concoction of chicken, limes and coriander, he has been heard to exclaim, 'Oh NO! I was hoping to have some of that for breakfast!' Nothing wrong, of course, with either rhubarb or chicken at breakfast time, and why shouldn't Eric's diet be as individual as the rest of him? Anyway, he's got it dead right – he does actually *have* breakfast in an age when an estimated quarter of the British workforce go to work on nothing more than a cup of tea, and most of the rest of us call a handful of over-refined, over-processed, over-sugared, over-priced particles of corn or rice a 'meal'. In honour of Eric, therefore, I have created the following recipe:

1 lb (500 g) rhubarb	1 handful of sultanas or raisins
1 cupful of orange juice	1 heaped tablespoon of sugar
1 teaspoon of powdered ginger	

Cut the rhubarb into 1" pieces. Chop the sultanas finely. Mix everything together. Stew very slowly in a covered saucepan, until the rhubarb is cooked.

Strain carefully, saving the juice for the topping. Place the fruit in an ovenproof dish.

Muesli topping:

8 oz (250 g) mixture of sunflower seeds, sesame seeds, green pumpkin seeds and wheatgerm
3 oz (80 g) chopped sultanas or raisins
the saved cooking juice

Mix together and spread over the cooked rhubarb. Bake at gas 4, 350° F, 180° C until golden brown and crispy, about 20-30 minutes.

Yoghurt-Custard Sauce:

Make a pint of custard, using either the egg custard or the packet custard method. Stir a tablespoonful of Greek yoghurt (or smatana or fromage frais) into each serving.

Enough for 4-6 helping. Eat for breakfast or anytime.

HOWELL DANIELS, Introduction to Eric Mottram's lecture '"What a place to sleep!": Intercultural and Countercultural Actions from 1950 in America'; given at the Institute of United States Studies' colloquium "A Permanent Etcetera: Engagements with America", 12 May 1990.

Well now ladies and gentlemen, we now come to the final session of the colloquium. When I asked Eric who he would like to chair he said "You, providing you agree not to tell the truth". I promised however to tell the truth – almost. And I'd like to begin with a story about long ago when the world and we were much younger and when we had rather more hair and rather more illusions about the nature of higher education; Eric and I attended a formal dinner in this university to mark the establishment of this Institute. The story which was told by the then American minister in London concerned the fact that on a Cunarder in the earlier years of this century there were the two best speakers in the world, Mark Twain and Chauncey Depew. The captain decided to put to the test what everyone was talking about and asked them both to speak after the dinner on the first night out. Chauncey Depew got up and in the opinion of those present gave the most brilliant and effective speech that they had ever heard. It had wit, humanity, compassion, humour, everything. He sat down to tumultuous applause. Twain then shambled to his feet and drawled "Well Mr Captain I am very pleased to have the opportunity to say a few words and I'm particularly glad to meet Mr Chauncey Depew again. In fact we met on deck for the first time this morning and we took a few strolls and the result of that was we agreed that he would write my speech and I would write his". And he sat down.

Now at this point I am tempted to sit down and say no more. But to do so would be to deprive me of the opportunity to celebrate the many years of friendship I have enjoyed with Eric and also to pay tribute to his long and greatly valued association with our Institute which in a small way we have sought to commemorate today.

A few years ago, some of you may remember, Arnold Goldman, when confronted by a similar task claimed that one could no more introduce Eric then one could present an elemental force of nature! And I am not even going to try. He is known to each and every one of you in this room and your presence testifies to the affection and high regard in which he is held. I would like to say however, that my own recollections of Eric go back almost thirty years to the early 1960s, when after war service in the Far East, three years at Cambridge and the necessary number of *Wanderjahre* in South East Asia, Switzerland and Holland he had settled into one of the first designated posts in American Literature in this country at King's College. And there he has taught for thirty years with one term off for good behaviour and a year as an ACLS Fellow in New York in the middle 1960s and that, I'm sure he would agree, was Eric's annus mirabilis. And interestingly he has given us the first of a two volume essay on this year in the Bulletin of our Former Students' Association. It's therefore entirely appropriate that today's proceedings should be in his honour because for 24 of these 30 years Eric has been a true and staunch friend of the Institute, regularly offering a seminar on American Cultural Studies on our MA programme. Ever willing to help either directly or indirectly with the advancement of the Institute's activities and reputation.

I think it's also true to say that he is now the sole in-post survivor of discussions in smoke-filled rooms of the 1960s in which the conception and gestation of the Institute took place. Certainly in his capacity as a member of our Committee of Management and more latterly our Advisory Committee he represents a rare and unbroken link with those years. Nevertheless for me today he is still essentially the same dynamic intellectual force that I remember marching into battle against entrenched ranks of prejudice and superstition, also known then as the Board of Studies in English.

The lineaments of the teacher and the scholar are sufficiently well known to you, those of the musician and cook perhaps less so. Dozens of Eric's former students now teach all over the world; his official list of publications must run to 10 or 12 single space A4 pages which cumulatively, I think, illustrate the drastic intelligence and the informed enjoyment which he brings to both his reading and his writing. But standing here, I would very briefly like to draw attention to another aspect of his intellectual and pedagogical role and that is the, to my mind, quite extraordinarily generous way in which over the years he has constantly made his energy and his resources available to all. Whether institutionalised in the form of a CNAA, or external examining or more immediately and directly, to any interested inquirer -be he or she a fugitive from inadequate supervision in universities considerably older than this- or a mere member of his many audiences in Budapest or Philadelphia, Paris – which recently held a series of readings and lectures in his honour – Paris or Hyderabad.

This openness to experience, together with his capacity for friendship brings to mind another Eric with whom I think I am probably the most familiar here. And this is the Trans-Severn Maritime Eric, who in the last fifteen years or so has developed a deep affection – which I think amounts to love – for my native Pembrokeshire, where hill and cliff and sea and, I feel, restaurant all acknowledge his august presence.

And from a whole quiver full of memories I would, with your indulgence, like to pluck but one and it really stems from a photograph that shows Eric entering an opalescent sea in late afternoon flanked by my two daughters. Earlier that day he had pointed out to him a seaweed which is used for the making of that delectable comestible lava bread. But before he could be told that it was customary for the seaweed to be boiled for eight hours, preferably with a ham hock, Eric had plucked a frond from a rock, ate it with obvious relish and announced "Delicious!" to his startled audience. I remember this because I think that was the year in which he published his aleatory sequence of poems *A Precipice of Fishes.* A small volume which on one level illustrated the truth of Bongo's dictum "If you can kill a snake with it, it ain't art," but at another level it illustrated the extraordinarily productive meeting of sea, land and poet. And since he dedicated this sequence of poems to me, somewhat feebly I remember responding with a spasm of doggerel in reply based upon the photograph of Eric entering the sea with my two daughters. As I remember as opposed to his skilled verse mine read something like this: "Now flanked by Naiads slim and serene/ The Poet enters the watery Stream/ Protean Eric braves the waves forlorn/ To hear old Triton blow his wreathed Horn/ Who e'er attentive to the Poet's wishes/ Now provides a Precipice of Fishes."

More recent memories include this first encounter with a genuine Mabinogion fog upon the Preseli hills and his impeccable behaviour as a latter day cavalier of the rose. But the world I fear is not yet ready to receive details of these exploits. I have to report however that on his last visit it was at least three days before Eric was seen to open a book – on 14th century Welsh prosody. Now whatever that evidence may quite falsely suggest it is of course quite inconceivable that this most pre-eminent of voices on American Cultural Studies could be either lulled or stilled. It is in other words inconceivable that Eric should retire whatever the Government, the Inland Revenue or this University may decree.

All of us who know this most multifarious of men will I'm sure readily agree that here we have a person who will never go gentle into the good night of flaccid retirement. And to vary my poets, you don't have to peer too closely to see that the not so ancient eyes are glittering and gay. Released from such pressing sub-lunary concerns as yet another tutorial on Gatsby [Eric: "Oh God, yes!"] Eric more than most of us has enviable new fields in which to discharge his creative and his critical energies and in so doing, continue to enrich and enhance our lives. Throughout the day he has with commendable patience hovered on our battlements as it were. And I am all too conscious that with these few words I have further delayed his right and proper move to centre stage. His talk will bring the colloquium to an end and I would like to thank him now in advance not only for his contribution but also the generous assistance he has given in planning the day. And if you wish to ask questions either here afterwards or in the other room in the bar, I am quite sure that Eric will be happy to talk to you. So, cometh the hour, cometh the man; ladies and gentlemen, friends and colleagues, with admiration and affection: Eric.

North and South gratefully acknowledges the following individuals and institutions without whom this book could not have been produced.

BENEFACTORS

David Annwn, Caroline and Tony Benn, Robert J. Bertholf, Branch Redd, Clive Bush, Dale Carter, Hennig Cohen, Ulla Dydo, Ken Edwards, Leslie A. Fiedler, Allen Fisher, Wendy Stallard Flory, Gary Frame, Diana Gravill, Robert Hampson, Peter Hodgkiss, Pierre Joris, Martin A. Kayman, Peter and Stella Makin, David Murray, Jeff Nuttall, John Page, John Porter, the Public House Bookshop, Erwin Rose, Will Rowe, Jerome Rothenberg, Robert Saffer, Barry Sheerman, Peterjon and Yasmin Skelt, Nathaniel Tarn, Lawrence Upton, Stephen Want, John and Mary Whiting, Ted and Joan Wilentz, T. Wignesan, Jonathan Williams, Shamoon Zamir, Anon.

SUBSCRIBERS

Basil Bunting Poetry Centre, Neil Crawford, R. J. Ellis, Fred Hunter, A. Robert Lee, Jim Mays, Oriel Bookshop, Pig Press, Gavin Selerie, Drake Stutesman, Wilson, Keppel and Betty

NOTES ON CONTRIBUTORS

GILBERT ADAIR ran the Sub-Voicive series of poetry readings in London 1980-1992 and now teaches at the University of Singapore. His collections of poetry include *Signs of Life* (1982), *Steakweasel* (1987) and *Jizz Rim* (1993-4).

DAVID ANNWN's recent publications include *the spirit / that kiss: New and Selected Poems 1973-1993* (1993). "This morning I dreamt I was at a party, hearing Eric's voice from another room. I'd been asked to include a brief bio on a card for him. One voice said: Write that you are a borderer, one of the Bards. Another voice said, Look at this photo. It was of Eric, surrounded by students, some sitting, standing, somewhere in the Mid-West on a rocky hillside. They were from all over the world and in high spirits. One woman sat with her back to a small fountain. They sat on the edge of a great landscape, smiling. And I heard Eric's laughter, slipped the photo in the card and went to show it to him."

JOHN ASHBERY was born in 1927 and currently teaches at Bard College in Rochester, New York. His recent books of poetry include *April Galleons* (1987), *Flow Chart* (1991), *Hotel Lautreaument* (1992), and *And the Stars Were Shining* (1994).

MARC ATKINS, photographer and performance artist, was born in 1962. He has lived, worked and exhibited in the UK, Netherlands, Italy and North America.

TONY BAKER lives in Derbyshire, edits the magazine FIGS and works as a musician and freelance naturalist. His most recent collection is *Scrins* (1989).

ROBERT BANK is an "ex King's College student, ex painter, ex publisher, ex gallery owner, ex meritus".

IAN BELL holds a Personal Chair in American Literature at the University of Keele. He has written widely on American poetry and fiction of the nineteenth and twentieth centuries, and his books include *Critic as Scientist: The Modernist Poetics of Ezra Pound* (1981); *Henry James and the Past: Readings into Time* (1991); *Washington Square: Styles of Money* (1993) and *The Best of O. Henry* (1993).

CHARLES BERNSTEIN co-edited L=A=N=G=U=A=G=E and now teaches at the State University of New York at Buffalo. Recent publications include *Content's Dream: Essays 1975-1984* (1985), *The Sophist* (1986) and *Dark City* (1994).

ELIOT BERRY lives in New York. His books include a novel and a book on the American writer, John Hawkes, which emerged from a Ph.D. dissertation directed by Eric at King's College, in 1978. In 1992, Henry Hold & Company published his third book, non-fiction.

ROBERT J. BERTHOLF is Curator of The Poetry and Rare Book Collection at the University of New York at Buffalo.

ALOK BHALLA got his Ph.D. from Kent State University and teaches at the Central Institute of English and Foreign Languages, Hyderabad, India. He has recently edited *Stories About the Partition of India* in three volumes. His other published works include *The Cartographers of Hell: Essays on the Gothic Novel and the Social History of England in the 19th Century, An Introduction to Latin American Literature* and *Images of Rural India in the 20th Century* (co-edited with Peter Bumke). He has translated many novels, stories and poems into English.

CHRIS BROOKEMAN is Principal Lecturer in English and American Studies at the University of Westminster. He has worked with Eric on several poetry conferences and is the co-founder with Eric of the William Bendix Appreciation Society.

WILLIAM S. BURROUGHS was born in St. Louis, Missouri in 1914. He studied at Harvard, travelled around Europe between the wars and worked odd-jobs in New York City in the early 1940s. He later travelled extensively in North Africa and Europe, living during the 1950s and 1960s in Tangiers, Paris and London; he now lives in Kansas. His books include *Junkie* (1953), *The Naked Lunch* (1959), *The Place of Dead Roads* (1984), and *The Adding Machine: Collected Essays* (1985).

CLIVE BUSH is a Reader in American Literature at King's College London. His publications include *The Dream of Reason* (1977), *shifts in undreamt time* (1989), *Halfway to Revolution: Investigation and Crisis in the Works of Henry Adams, William James and Gertrude Stein* (1991).

RICHARD CADDEL's latest publication is *Ground* (1994). He is also Associate Editor of *Basil Bunting Complete Poems* (1994). He, "like many, owes a huge debt to Eric Mottram for serious and generous criticism and support in the poetry biz over many years".

DALE CARTER completed master's and doctoral theses at the Institute of United States Studies, London under Eric's supervision. He has lectured on American History at Warwick University and since 1989 has taught American studies at the University of Aarhus, Denmark. He helped Eric prepare *Blood on the Nash Ambassador: Investigation in American Culture* (1989) for publication. His own books include *The Final Frontier: The Rise and Fall of the American Rocket State* (1988) and *Cracking the Ike Age* (edited, 1993).

CRIS CHEEK: "Eric's energetic presence as editor of POETRY REVIEW, as curator of the King's College Reading series and of the Polytechnic of Central London Modern British Poetry Conferences introduced me to an extraordinary range and dynamic of poetic practices and processes. And did so at a time when I needed the challenge and stimulation of diversity most. I had opted out of formal re-education early and set off along slightly less clearly defined paths. I was re-discovering that process of tentatively stumbling. His knack was to 'get poets going'. Since then it has been the essential strangeness, the curiosity, of his encouragement that has perhaps encouraged me the most."

PAULA CLAIRE has been involved in sound and visual poetry since the early 1960s. She performs, exhibits and publishes her work internationally. She celebrated 30 years of Poetry at The Arts Council Poetry Library, South Bank Centre, London in 1991, with a book, introduction by Eric, performance, workshop and cassette. She is Visiting Lecturer in the School of Visual Arts, Music and Publishing, Oxford Brookes University. She founded and curates The International Concrete Poetry Archive in Oxford.

THOMAS A. CLARK was born in Greenock, Scotland in 1944. He lives in Nailsworth, Gloucestershire where with his wife Laurie he runs Moschatel Press and the Cairn Gallery, a centre for contemporary art. Recent collections of poetry include: *The Tempers of Hazard* and *Tormentil and Bleached Bones* (both 1993).

DAVID COOK is a painter and printmaker. Originally trained as a textile designer at Bradford College and Royal College of Art, he began painting on a full time basis in the early 1980s and has exhibited works throughout UK, Europe, USA and Asia. He recently exhibited in the first International Frafiek Biennale, Maastricht, Holland 1993. He lives and works in North Yorkshire.

JULIAN COWLEY is a lecturer in the Department of English at the University of Luton. He has published a number of articles on American fiction.

RICHARD CUPIDI runs the Public House Bookshop in Brighton.

HOWELL DANIELS (1932-1993) was Secretary of the Institute of United State Studies in London for 25 years until his retirement in 1990.

JOHN DAVIES is Anglo-Welsh. He was a student of Eric in the 1960s.

PETER DONNELLY is the Dean of the School of Graphic Design at the London College of Printing. He has created graphics for most of Eric's books since 1973.

KEN EDWARDS was born in 1950. He lives in London and edited REALITY STUDIOS for many years. He runs Reality Street Editions with Wendy Mulford. His publications include *Drumming & Poems* (1982), *Intensive Care* (1986) and *Good Science, Poems 1983-1991* (1993).

ELAINE FEINSTEIN has written eleven novels, most recently *Dreamers* (1994) and nine books of poems. Her *Selected Poems* were published in September 1994.

LAWRENCE FERLINGHETTI runs the City Lights Bookshop in San Francisco. His many books include *A Coney Island of The Mind* (1958), *Endless Life: Selected Poems* (1981) and *Seven Days in Nicaragua Libre* (1986).

LESLIE FIEDLER was born in New Jersey in 1917. He taught at Montana State University for two decades and is now Professor of English at the State University of New York at Buffalo. His many books include *Love and Death in the American Novel* (1960), *Waiting for the End* (1964), *The Stranger in Shakespeare* (1972) and *Fiedler on the Roof* (1991).

PETER FINCH was born in Cardiff, Wales where he still lives. He runs he Oriel Bookshop as he has for twenty years. He is a former editor and was part of the great Poetry Society push back in the 1970s that flung Eric onto the editing stage with his ground breaking run of POETRY REVIEW. Peter's poetry is collected in *Selected Poems* (Poetry Wales Press) and in his two more recent titles *Poems for Ghosts* (Seren) and *Five Hundred Cobbings* (Writers Forum).

ALLEN FISHER was born in 1944 and has been writing poetry since 1962. A printer, painter, publisher and editor, he has produced over one hundred chapbooks and books of poetry, graphics and art documentation. He currently edits SPANNER, and lives in Hereford where he is Curriculum Co-ordinator and Lecturer at the Herefordshire College of Art and Design. His last two shows of painting were in King's Manor Gallery, York 1993 and in Hereford City Art Gallery 1994. His most recent books are *Civic Crime* (1994) and *Fizz* (1994).

ROY FISHER was born in Birmingham in 1930. His books include *Poems 1955-80* (1980), *A Furnace* (1986) and *It Follows That* (1994).

SANDRA FISHER (1947-1994) was born in New York City and moved to London in 1971. Public collections holding her work include the British Museum, the Victoria and Albert Museum, London and the Metropolitan Museum of Art, New York. Her pictures have been published with poems and translations by Thomas Meyer in *Sappho* (1982), *Sonnets and Tableaux* (1987) and *Monotypes & Tracings* (1994). Posters have been made from paintings commissioned by the London Underground (1989 and 1991) and by Heineken's, Amsterdam (1993).

WENDY STALLARD FLORY received a Ph.D. in American Literature in 1970, has been assistant professor at Rutgers University and the University of Pennsylvania and is now professor of English at Purdue University, Indiana. She has published *Ezra Pound and The Cantos: A Record of Struggle* (1980) and *The American Ezra Pound* and is now working on *A New Symbol Criticism: Symbolic Characters and the American Romance*. She is married with two children, now 24 and 21.

GARY FRAME teaches English and American Literature at Langara College in Vancouver, British Columbia.

ULLI FREER lives in London. His most recent publication is *Sandpoles* (1991).

ALLEN GINSBERG was born in 1926 in Paterson, New Jersey. He co-founded the Jack Kerouac School of Disembodied Poetics in Boulder, Colorado in 1974. Recent books include *Mind Breaths* (1978), *Plutonium Ode* (1982) and *Collected Poems 1947-1980* (1984).

WOLFGANG GÖRTSCHACHER teaches contemporary literature in English at the Institute for English and American Studies at the University of Salzburg, Austria. His book *The Little Magazines in Great Britain 1939-1992* was published in 1993.

ROBERT HAMPSON is senior lecturer at Royal Holloway College, University of London. His recent publications include *a human measure* (1989), *Unicorns: Seven Studies in Velocity* (1989) and *New British Poetries: The Scope of the Possible* (co-edited with Peter Barry, 1993).

BOBBIE LOUISE HAWKINS has had seven collections of short stories and poetry published as well as two novels of which the latest is *The Sanguine Breast of Margaret* (1992). She teaches in the Master of Fine Arts programme at Naropa Institute in Boulder, Colorado and runs the Bijou Theatre there.

PETER HODGKISS published POETRY INFORMATION magazine and ran the Galloping Dog Press for many years.

MICHAEL HREBENIAK "had the good luck to meet Eric Mottram early in my undergraduate career. After five years clerical imbecility world opened up – the beginnings of honest work. Now researching a PhD thesis on New York scene, 1945-60, and teaching 20th century art and literature at the Royal Academy of Music. Have also taught jazz history for the WEA, published jazz articles and played tenor saxophone. Eric continues to be true friend and mentor."

JOSEF JAŘAB, was born in 1937 in Czechoslovakia, graduate of Palacký University, Olomouc, Czech Republic. Studied and taught at various other universities in his own country and abroad (including University of London, NYU, Brandeis, Harvard). He is currently Professor of English and American Literature at his alma mater where he was elected Rector during the revolution of 1989. He has lectured and published widely at home and in other countries; his special interest is focused on modern American poetry and American ethnic writers, above all African-Americans. He met with Eric Mottram in 1967 as a student in his class at the Institute of United States Studies in London; they chatted often at King's College and in pubs within the vicinity. They met again in 1980 at an EAAS conference in Budapest and spent a long time talking "whilst walking down a boulevard and eating bread and cheese and drinking wine from a bottle like two bums". At the occasion of another EAAS conference, in London at Easter 1990, he visited Eric at Herne Hill to boast of the victorious revolution, of his own modest "from dissident to president" story, and of his achievements in writing and scholarship.

PIERRE JORIS left Luxembourg at eighteen and has since lived in the USA, Great Britain, North Africa and France. He teaches at The State University of New York at Albany. He has published over twenty books of poetry; most recently, *Winnetou Old, Turbulence* and *The Irritation Ditch,* as well as several anthologies and many volumes of translations, both into English and into French. He collaborated with Jerome Rothenberg on *pppppp: Selected Writings of Kurt Schwitters* (1993). He is currently finishing a new book of poems, *Facing the Plaza, If Not The Music* and collaborating with Jerome Rothenberg on another anthology.

MARTIN A. KAYMAN is a Professor at the Instituto de Estudos Ingleses at the University of Coimbra, Portugal. "Like so many others, I met Eric as a graduate student. Unlike many others, however, I was not fortunate enough to be his supervisee (although fortunate I was in my supervisor).

Nonetheless I was privileged to enjoy, however briefly and occasionally, his generosity and encouragement for the young tyro's effort to prove him and the rest of the more informed world wrong. So much so that I once dared to send him some verses for his appreciation. His response was to try to persuade me to abandon my clear attachment to the left margin. Was my difficulty lack of courage, or stubborn conviction? Eric is a man of estuaries and (therefore) openings; I live and work on the left-hand (but right-wing) margin of Europe. Cast off from here, and who knows where you'll end up (they say there's a continent out there – and that Eric Mottram has mapped it). Meanwhile, I sit in my chair on the Lusitanian beach, and admire."

ROBERT KELLY teaches at Bard College in New York State and has had over fifty collections of poetry published.

R B KITAJ was born in Ohio, USA and has lived in the UK for many years. Recent exhibitions in London include a retrospective at The Tate Gallery, recent work at the Marlborough Gallery and prints at the Victoria and Albert Museum.

ALLEN DE LOACH is a poet, prose writer, photographer, multi-media performer, producer and director of a TV series entitled Video-Poetics for Public Television. He as edited and published Intrepid Press books, Intrepid Magazine and the Beau Fleuve series of books since 1963. He has published Eric Mottram's work since the mid-1960s, including the first edition of Mottram's *William Burroughs: The Algebra of Need* in 1971. He first met Eric at the State University of New York at Buffalo in 1966 where Eric and Basil Bunting were visiting professors. "On the Occasion of Eric Mottram's 70th Birthday" is derived from a trip Eric made to the Hopi Reservation in Shungopavi, Second Mesa, Arizona in the spring of 1979 where De Loach was living with his adopted family. He writes: "Eric is a major contributor to English Literature and the foremost literary critic of English and American Literature."

JACKSON MAC LOW was born in 1922 and grew up in Chicago and Kenilworth, Illinois. His musical compositions have been performed in Europe and the USA. His recent publications include *The Virginia Woolf Poems* (1985), *Representative Works 1938-1985* (1986).

THOMAS MEYER was born in 1947 in Seattle, Washington. His books include: *The Bang Book* (1971), *The Umbrella of Aesculapius* (1975), *Sappho* (1982), *Sonnets and Tableaux* (1987) and *Monotypes and Tracings / German Romantics* (1994), the latter three with pictures by Sandra Fisher.

DAVID MOODY is Professor of English and American Literature at the University of York.

WENDY MULFORD lives and works in Suffolk as a writer, teaches part-time in Cambridge and runs Reality Street Editions with Ken Edwards. She edited the *Virago Book of Love Poetry* (1990). Most recent collections of poetry include *Nevrazumitelny* (1991), *The Bay of Naples* (1992). *East Anglian Sequences* is forthcoming in 1994-95. She has an unpublished book on Russian revolutionary women painters and is about to start on a collaborative project, a book of women saints.

JEFF NUTTALL is a poet, visual artist, jazz musician and actor. His books include *Bomb Culture, Scenes and Dubs,* and *What Happened to Jackson.*

Emeritus Professor **JOHN PAGE** was Professor of Building Science in the Faculty of Architectural Studies in the University of Sheffield for 25 years. He recently was the initiating Director of the Cambridge Interdisciplinary Environmental Centre. He has published some 200 papers and books dealing with environment and architecture, and worked for UN agencies on environment and building issues. He was founding Chairman of the UK Section of International Solar Energy Society and received the top International Award of the International Society for his work on solar energy.

SIMON PETTET is the author of *Lyrical Poetry, 21 Love* and most recently, with Rudy Burckhardt, *Talking Pictures.* He studied with Eric in London in the 1970s at the Institute of United States Studies and currently resides in New York where he is researching that city's culture and where he himself is an active part of it.

TOM PICKARD was born in Newcastle upon Tyne in 1946. His books include *Hero Dust, Guttersnipe* and *Jarrow March.*

JOHN PORTER teaches at King's College London. His books include a parallel text edition of *Beowulf* (1975) and *The Riddles from the Exeter Book* (1978).

ELAINE RANDELL was born in London in 1951. She edited AMAZING GRACE magazine in the 1960s and Secret Books in the 1970s. Her books include *Beyond All Other* and *Gut Reaction. Faulty Mothering* is forthcoming.

TOM RAWORTH has read widely throughout Europe and the USA and lives in Cambridge. His many publications include *Tottering State* (1984 and 1988) and *The Mosquito and The Moon* (1994).

ERWIN ROSE is active in progressive politics in the USA; he worked as an aide to the American socialist leader Michael Harrington, as a community organiser in the Bronx NY, and served as a legislative aide in the New York State senate 1988-93. He studied with Eric at King's College 1982-83 under the University of Pennsylvania programme.

JEROME ROTHENBERG is the author of over fifty books of poetry including *Poems for the Game of Silence, Poland/1931, New Selected Poems 1970-1985, Khurbn,* and *The Lorca Variations.* He has also edited six ground breaking anthologies of experimental and traditional poetry (including *Technicians of the Sacred, Shaking the Pumpkin, A Big Jewish Book, America a Prophecy*) and has been actively engaged in poetry and performance since the late 1950s. With Pierre Joris he is currently working on a two-volume global anthology of twentieth-century avant-garde writing: *Poems for the Millennium.*

WILL ROWE is Professor of Latin American Cultural Studies at King's College London. His publications include a volume of Antonia Cisneros' poems, *At Night the Cats* (1985) and the critical study *Juan Rulfo* (1987).

ROB SAFFER studied with Eric at King's College under the University of Pennsylvania programme in 1982-83.

IAN SEIDERMAN "was born in Philadelphia in 1962 and grew up in New York. At the age of 20 I had brain surgery performed on me by Dr Mottram. I now spend my days in Geneva, ranting something about 'human rights'."

HUBERT SELBY JR was born in Brooklyn in 1926. The British publishers of his first novel *Last Exit to Brooklyn* were successfully prosecuted for obscenity at the Old Bailey, London in 1967, a verdict which was overturned on appeal on a technicality. His other books include *The Room* and *The Demon.*

GAVIN SELERIE was born in Hampstead, London in 1949 and still lives in north-west London. He teaches at the Centre for Extra-Mural Studies, Birkbeck College. He worked with Eric Mottram on *The Riverside Interview 4: Jerome Rothenberg* (1984). Other writings include studies of Charles Olson and the Scottish playwright Tom McGrath. Poetry includes *Azimuth* (1984), *Southam Street* (1991) and *Tilting Square* (1992). Major work-in-progress: *Roxy,* parts of which have been published in magazines and in the anthology *Ten British Poets* (1993).

BILL SHERMAN was born and raised in Philadelphia. He first came to Europe in 1962, and first lived in London from 1964-65. He gained his Ph.D. in English and American Literature at The State University of New York at Buffalo. He has taught at the University of Hull and the University College of Wales at Aberystwyth. He edits and publishes Branch Redd Books, and co-directed with Theodora Chichy the short film, *Maximus to Himself,* based on the poem by Charles Olson. His publications include *The Horses of Gwyddno Garanhir* (1976), *Tahitian Journals* (1990) and the forthcoming *Polynesian Threnody.*

COLIN SIMMS was born in 1939, "merely one of those many Eric has guided and helped significantly. Live warm poet and critic and teacher; the whole one patient example and a test, proven good and true friend. Persisting with my long stubborn-nesses, he has pruned and promoted, and I hope he lives long enough to see some worthwhile fruit out of this windy thick thicket!"

IAIN SINCLAIR lives in East London. He is the author of a book of poems and speculations, *Lud Heat.* And the novels *Whitechappell, Scarlet Tracings, Downriver, Radon Daughters.*

PETERJON SKELT co-founded North and South in 1986 and has designed all of the North and South books. His drawings have been published in *King Saturn's Book* with poems by David Annwn (1987) and *American Shore* (1993). His latest solo exhibition was in 1993 at the Wakefield Arts Centre, Yorkshire.

YASMIN SKELT co-founded North and South, and the multi-media publishers Solaris. For Solaris she is producing the KNOWING WORDS: CONTEMPORARY WRITERS series of video documentaries, on Bobbie Louise Hawkins (1993) and Elaine Randell (1994) to date.

NATHANIEL TARN is a poet, translator, editor, critic and specialist in Highland Maya studies and the sociology of Buddhist institutions. He has published some twenty five books of poetry and translation, mainly from Spanish, French and Maya. His main works are *The Beautiful Contradictions* (1969), *Lyrics for the Bride of God* (1975), *The House of Leaves* (1976), *Seeing America First* (1989) and *Views from the Weaving Mountain, Selected Essays in Poetics and Anthropology* (1991). His poetry has been translated into over fifteen foreign languages. Tarn lives in northwest Santa Fe, New Mexico USA.

LAWRENCE UPTON: "Born 1949. Artist/poet. Professionally a lecturer in Computing. Presently, editing / publishing RWC magazine and running the Sub-Voicive readings in London. "Letter to Eric" is part of "Messages to Silence" a very long sequence of epistolary poems some of which have been published. I knew Eric long before he became my university lecturer – and that was for five weeks only! But the university work is only one type of teaching: I find him exemplary in his endeavour and human in his friendship, a giddying and creative mixture of the domestic and teleological!"

ANNE WALDMAN was Director of St Mark's Poetry project, New York and a founder and co-director of the Jack Kerouac School of Disembodied Poetics in Boulder, Colorado. Her publications include *Fast Speaking Woman* (1975) and *Helping the Dreamer: New and Selected Poems 1966-88* (1989).

STEPHEN WANT is a "student and grateful friend of Eric Mottram since 1982"; an editor of TALUS, and Lecturer in American Studies at West London Institute, Brunel University.

JOHN WHITING is a free-lance sound designer and recordist based in London and working throughout Europe and America. His recent history of the early days of KPFA, the listener-sponsored radio station in Berkeley, California (published in THE DOLPHIN, Aarhus University Press) is to be expanded into a CD ROM book.

MARY WHITING is an author, journalist and cookery teacher who specializes in healthy gourmet food, particularly for young children. She wrote *The Nursery Food Book* with Tim Lobstein of The Food Commission, and they have been commissioned by the same publisher to write another. Over a quarter of a century ago Eric was Best Man at the Whitings' wedding. None of them ever got over it.

T. WIGNESAN, "a Stateless Person, expelled from Malaysia, his birthplace, now works as a researcher-comparatist in Paris for the French National Centre for Scientific Research (C.N.R.S.) at the Ecole des Hautes Etudes en Sciences Sociales. Writes poetry, short stories, essays, novels and criticism, mainly in English, and is the founder-editor of the bi-lingual JOURNAL OF COMPARATIVE POÏETICS / REVUE DE PÖIÉTIQUE COMPARÉE."

JOAN STEEN WILENTZ is a professional science writer at the National Institutes of Health and Chief of the Planning and Legislation Section of the National Institute of Dental Research, USA. She also writes book reviews, was the first woman editor of POPULAR SCIENCE MONTHLY and wrote the book *The Senses of Man* (1968).

TED WILENTZ has been a bookseller, editor and co-publisher of Corinth Books, a literary press. He is a member of PEN American Centre and of MENSA.

JONATHAN WILLIAMS is a poet, essayist, photographer and publisher of the Jargon Society. Recent publications include *Metafours for Mysophobes* (1989), *Eight Days in Eire* (1990), *Quantulumcumque* (1991) and *Jonathan Williams' Quote Book* (1994).

INDEX OF CONTRIBUTORS

CONTEMPORARY LITERATURE FROM NORTH AND SOUTH

Poetry

David Annwn, *King Saturn's Book*
David Annwn, *The Spirit / That Kiss: New and Selected Poems*
Richard Caddel, *Against Numerology*
Kelvin Corcoran, *The Next Wave*
Lee Harwood, *Rope Boy to The Rescue*
Geraldine Monk, *The Sway of Precious Demons: Selected Poems*
Eric Mottram, *Selected Poems*
Frances Presley, *The Sex of Art*
Lisa Raphals, *What Country*
Catherine Walsh, *Short Stories,*
Jonathan Williams, *Metafours for Mysophobes*

Prose

Bobbie Louise Hawkins, *The Sanguine Breast of Margaret*
Elaine Randell, *Gut Reaction*

Interviews

ed. Peterjon Skelt, *Prospect Into Breath*

Festschrift

Alive in Parts of this Century: Eric Mottram at 70